D1287066

THE NEW ALLIANCE

AMERICA'S R&D CONSORTIA

DAN DIMANCESCU

JAMES BOTKIN

BALLINGER PUBLISHING COMPANY
A subsidiary of Harper & Row, Publishers, Inc.
Cambridge, Massachusetts 02138

Copyright © 1986 by James W. Botkin and Dan Dimancescu. All rights reserved. No part of this publication may be reproduced, stored in a retrieval system, or transmitted in any form or by any means, electronic, mechanical, photocopy, recording or otherwise, without the prior written consent of the publisher.

International Standard Book Number: 0-88730-046-4

Library of Congress Catalog Card Number: 86-20613

Library of Congress Cataloging-in-Publication Data

Dimancescu, Dan.
  The new alliance.

  Includes index.
  1. Research, Industrial—United States. 2. Research institutes—United States.
I. Botkin, James W.   II. Title.
T176.D47   1986   338.97306   86-20613

                              ISBN 0-88730-046-4

BST
R

424.46

Contents

Part I – CONSORTIA

What Would It Take?
Three Consortia
Rearranging the Pieces

Global Competition
New Technologies
Push or Pull?

Part II – FRAMING THE QUESTIONS

Part III – THE MECHANICS

Preface

Important beyond its skillful understanding of the alliances themselves, this work probes the underlying forces and the changing nature of business in a world where knowledge, as an asset, has surged in importance relative to the more traditional view of fiscal or physical assets.

With the increased status of the *knowledge asset* in business has come the need to explore new techniques for finding, assimilating, maintaining, and creating knowledge. Part of this search has brought about the many "new alliances" between industry, universities, and government described in this book.

There are those who believe that the partnership involved in these "new alliances" represent the first modest but critical step for our nation on a journey back to competitive vitality in a global economy—a journey both for our "basic" and our so-called "growth" industries. But a more important step will be the changes within our corporations as they evolve into knowledge-based-organizations. Those that change will be driven by new processes, policies, and procedures for managing and owning knowledge as a corporate asset. As important as such changes are to our future competitiveness, it is this part that the authors say is missing in the consortia movement of the 80s. Ironically, it may be this omission that points us in the right direction.

The subject of university and industry "joint projects" is certainly not new. In my own brief career, I can reach back to 1974 when I was Director of the Rockwell International Science Center. I spoke of the subject that year to the Annual Meeting of the Society of Research Administrators on my corporate perspective and in a course entitled "Turning Science into Business" at UCLA's School of Management. In my comments I referred to examples in microwave electronics, hydrogen embrittlement, and Project Clean Air in California. Each example involved many of the country's leading scientists and foremost universities. In this talk, I used a relatively controversial phrase: "science systems integrator." It meant a far more direct and dynamic manner than was customary. More conventional methods relied mostly on reading academic publications. And it was more direct even than the traditional consulting relationships between industry and universities. We were greatly concerned then about the flow of knowledge from the university into the industrial environment. We still are today. What is different today is that the economic climate is clouded by deteriorated trade balances and surprisingly swift losses of market shares in key industries such as semiconductors.

Although, it can be said that the subject of this book is not new it can be argued that it has never before been so strategically important to our future. We experimented in the seventies. We are doing it again in the 1980s. The job now is to move new concepts into the world of production —both in manufacturing and service industries. We must do more than experiment if we are to reach our full potential in an unforgiving era of global competition where knowledge itself must be managed for success.

*Dr. Terry Loucks,** Vice President for Technology
Norton Company, Worcester, Massachusetts*

*Also: Panel Member: National Science Foundation Engineering Research Centers; Panel Chairman: National Research Council Materials Science and Engineering Study

R&D CONSORTIA STUDIED

	Name and Location	*Founded*
ATHENA	PROJECT ATHENA Massachusetts Institute of Technology (MIT) Cambridge, Massachusetts [includes reference to CMU–ITC with IBM]	1983
CAOT	CENTER FOR ADVANCED OPTICAL TECHNOLOGY—A New York State Center for Advanced Technology Institute of Optics, University of Rochester, Rochester, New York	1983
CCR	CENTER FOR CERAMICS RESEARCH—An Advanced Technology Center of New Jersey Rutgers University, New Brunswick, New Jersey	1982
CIDMAC	COMPUTER INTEGRATED DESIGN, MANUFACTURING, AND AUTOMATION CENTER Purdue University, West Lafayette, Indiana	1982
CII	CENTER FOR INDUSTRIAL INNOVATION Rensselaer Polytechnic Institute, Troy, New York	1978
CIS	CENTER FOR INTEGRATED SYSTEMS Stanford University, Palo Alto, California	1980
CST	CORPORATION FOR SCIENCE & TECHNOLOGY Indianapolis, Indiana	1982
ITI	INDUSTRIAL TECHNOLOGY INSTITUTE Ann Arbor, Michigan	1982
MEAC	MANUFACTURING ENGINEERING APPLICATIONS CENTER Worcester Polytechnic Institute, Worcester, Massachusetts	1981
MEC	MICROELECTRONICS CENTER Massachusetts Technology Park Corporation, Westborough, Massachusetts	1982

R&D CONSORTIA STUDIED

	Name and Location	*Founded*
MCC	MICROELECTRONIC AND COMPUTER TECHNOLOGY CORPORATION Austin, Texas	1983
MCNC	MICROELECTRONICS CENTER OF NORTH CAROLINA Research Triangle Park, North Carolina	1980
RI	ROBOTICS INSTITUTE Carnegie-Mellon University, Pittsburgh, Pennsylvania	1979
RRC	ROBOTICS RESEARCH CENTER University of Rhode Island	1971

ADVISORS

Mr. Erich Bloch, Director—National Science Foundation

Mr. Edmund Cranch, President—Wang Institute

Dr. Pat Crecine, Vice President for Academic Affairs—Carnegie-Mellon University

Dr. Richard Cyert, President—Carnegie-Mellon University

Mr. Peter Ellis, Program Officer—W.K. Kellogg Foundation

Mr. Herbert Fusfeld, Director—Center for Science and Technology Policy, Graduate School of Public Administration at New York University

Mr. George Herbert, President—Research Triangle Institute

Mr. Robert R. Inman, Chairman and CEO—Microelectronics and Computer Technology Corporation

Dr. John Linvill, Co-Director—Center for Integrated Systems at Stanford University

Dr. Terry Loucks, Vice President for Technology—Norton Company

Mr. Frank Newman, President—Education Commission of the States

Dr. Lois Peters—Center for Science & Technology Policy, Graduate School of Public Administration at New York University

Prof. James Solberg—School of Engineering at Purdue University

Mr. Ray Stata, President—Analog Devices, Inc.

Mr. Marc Tucker, Director—Carnegie Forum

Mr. John Wilson, Manager of Planning for Corporate R&D—Cincinnati Milacron

Dr. Henry Yang, Dean—School of Engineering at Purdue University

ACKNOWLEDGMENTS

Our work would not have been possible without the farsighted support of the Carnegie Corporation of New York. Alden Dunham, program officer at the foundation, was instrumental in generating funding support that allowed the authors to complete this work. Support of a project along these broad thematic lines was itself an experiment for the Corporation under a new program in Science, Technology, and the Economy. Avery Russell, also at the foundation, provided valued support instrumental in carrying this work through to final manuscript preparation.

Our advisors generously offered first-hand insight, commentary, and depth of their experience. They shared views in one-to-one meetings, a gathering in New York to review an early draft of this manuscript, letter exchanges, and phone calls. Many of their views are liberally quoted throughout the text. The conclusions, however, are ours—for better or worse. Our thanks also to Tom Cummings on our staff for research assistance and to David Hamlin for external background inquiries and research. And our special thanks to the staff at Ballinger Publishing whose faith in the prompt delivery of a publishable manuscript never flagged and whose professional insights added professional polish to roughened edges.

It is nice, too, not to have to say thank you to a secretary who would normally have the unforgiving task of typing and retyping notes, scribblings, and typographical errors. Instead, this book was made possible with the use of an exceedingly easy to use Wang word-processing system on loan from Wang Laboratories. It typed and retyped our numerous edits and re-edits without complaint, day and night. Our Wang symbolizes the practical pervasiveness of computer technology. In our case, it was in improving our personal productivity many fold, in accelerating deadlines, and in allowing our publisher to function more efficiently.

INTRODUCTION

The 1980s might be called America's "R&D consortia years." Collaborative research agreements between industry, government, and universities have proliferated. What their impact might be and what might be learned of their experiences to date prompted the background work that led to this book. You will find a fair dose of optimism, some reservations, and a hidden amount of trepidation in the chapters that follow. The trepidation arises from tackling a topic vast and complex in its reach.

Any discussion of alliances between industry and universities—even the narrower focus we chose of research and development consortia—encompasses a broad horizon: large and small businesses in a wide array of industries, varied academic institutions, a diverse collection of political actors, an astounding collection of technologies, and national or regional economic ambitions. There were also touchy questions as diverse as those of academic freedom and of industry bottom-line self-interest. And matters of political rivalry. How could we shed light on any single facet? Worse yet, could we expect to generalize implications, educational and economic, for an entire nation from so piecemeal a perspective?

What links these disparate parts is a perception of an economy at an impasse. Productivity has stalled. Clearly, something must change if the country is to remain vibrant and competitive. It is in this light that the new R&D consortia—*The New Alliance*—are a timely litmus test of America's future well-being. They are surely not the only test. Nor perhaps even the most important indicator. What these consortia do offer is an intimate glimpse into our culture's resilience and creativity. This comes largely in response to economic pressure induced by competent and aggressive foreign competitors.

We are aware, also, of the argument some might offer that there is nothing essentially new about industry, academe, and government working together. Indeed, they have been doing it for most of the century. But what is worth scrutiny is the closeness of the collaborations being crafted. In this respect, they are qualitatively different from anything in the past. In most cases industry and academe held themselves to an arm's-length "show me what you come up with" kind of relationship. As late as 1982, the National Science Foundation released an excellent and detailed report on "University-Industry Research Relationships" produced by Lois Peters and Herbert Fusfeld of the Center for Science and Technology Policy at New York University. Their study included a review of 464 university-industry interactions. They reported that "despite the current interest and activity in cooperative research, there are very few programs with extensive collaboration between university and industry scientists in research design and management. Out of 284 interactions we classified as cooperative, we believe that only 2 percent fall into this category of truly collaborative interaction." (See suggested readings at end of introduction for source.)

Our own interest in this subject goes back several years. It started with a book we co-authored with Ray Stata, president of Analog Devices, Inc., entitled *Global Stakes* (see suggested readings). Our research led us to conclude that as high-tech industries grew in importance, the nation was understating the strategic importance of its education resources, particularly its technical talent. Engineering departments went underfunded, and with academics underpaid, professors and students were easily lured away to higher paying industry jobs.

At that time, one of the more ambitious responses to this problem was the founding of the Semiconductor Research Cooperative (SRC) recently renamed as a Corporation. Spearheaded by IBM, it was evident then that the SRC's impact might far exceed expectations. So too, we concluded at that time, for the newly created Microelectronics Center of North Carolina, itself only a year old. That was 1982.

By the end of 1985, a lot had changed. Take consortia. Suddenly there were *five times* more. Obviously, something special was going on. In addition, the National Science Foundation started funding a new group of select Engineering Research Centers as government, industry, and university collaboratives. Although small in proportion to the NSF's total budget appropriations, this initiative had important long-term implications for the ways in which applied research would be carried out. But missing, so far, was a commitment on a scale that seemed commensurate with the problem. In *Global Stakes*, we had recommended a federal High-Technology Morrill Act—a $1 billion program to rebuild the nation's engineering departments. Half this amount, we proposed, would be matched by federal funds and the balance by state and industry resources. It was filed in the 98th Congress by Senators Paul Tsongas and John Stennis. Eventually, parts of the bill were absorbed into Title III of the Education and Economic Security Act signed into law by President Ronald Reagan. He then promptly avoided funding it while allowing defense expenditures to skyrocket.

The problem of funding promises to get worse as the federal government gets down to the business of reversing Reagan's $2 trillion deficit binge. Federal support to education is apt to decrease as are federal R&D funds. Some of the biggest losers will be America's research and engineering universities. Indeed, looked at from a global economic perspective the timing and nature of our national investments are squarely off the mark.

This point became clearer to us when, in 1984, we co-authored, also with Stata, *The Innovators* (see suggested readings), with a subtitle heralding the rediscovery of America's creative energy. High tech, we noted in several case studies, was moving swiftly into older industries giving them a new lease on life. But this same trend was creating even greater pressures on academe to produce talented technicians. We argued that the users of a new generation of high-tech tools had as much at stake in our education infrastructure as the makers of those tools—the high-tech industries themselves. All this put even more stress on tending to civilian R&D priorities, on upgrading our existing workforce and on creating new generations of able young people.

In the interim our national productivity stayed flat as other nations continued to surge forward in fields we thought untouchable. High-tech electronics was "ours" until Japan proved otherwise with such things as computers, optical fibers, or large scale semiconductor chips—and other new technologies. And now rapidly industrializing countries like South

Korea are appearing on the scene. All this means that much remains to be done if we are to regain lost ground.

For these reasons, the creation of an increasing number of R&D consortia acquired special significance. They were founded by industry executives, academics, or government leaders who shared a common recognition of the importance of high tech to our economy and of the vital role education plays as a foundation to our competitive strength. These leaders set out to bring new resources to universities and to create an atmosphere in which a new generation of skilled individuals could grow.

In the process, many of these arrangements affected "business as usual" in industry, academe and government. Problems had to be tackled differently and partners who otherwise might remain at arms' length had to rub shoulders. All this underscored a need for change. Managers would have to manage emerging technologies in new ways. Academics would have to cross narrowly prescribed boundaries of their intellectual disciplines. Government officials would have to alter regulatory constraints, create new incentives, and tend to the mounting pressures for protectionism. Against this backdrop, the consortia phenomenon of the 1980s came forward as a great experiment. In truly American style, it was unleashed without master blueprints or even a clear sense of the ultimate outcome.

This third book, *The New Alliance*, is a look into the possible future of the consortia experiment. We examined fourteen of them closely. We focused on electronics, manufacturing, robotics, and new materials consortia, although others in different technologies also could have been included had our time and resources permitted. Many of the consortia we studied are but a few years old. Most will take five or more years to prove themselves. And as might be expected because of the novelty of the experiment, our findings are tentative at best. But with the benefit of insights from a dedicated group of advisors, many of them founders or members of consortia, we were able to study these alliances and their relationship to the competitive strength of the economy. This book is a guidepost of their progress.

With a few exceptions, the material we present is based on discussions with numerous consortia participants and documentation they provided. They were interviewed over a period of about nine months in 1984 and 1985 at their workplaces throughout the nation. Factual data was updated again in early 1986.

Our findings are presented in four parts. *Part I* focuses on descriptions of the R&D consortium as a phenomenon. A few illustrative cases are spelled out and a brief historical context given. Their importance as forerunners of deeper changes in our society is suggested.

In *Part II* we outline three questions important to an understanding of consortia and some of their outcomes: (1) Who sets the agenda of research? (2) How is the transfer of technology managed? (3) Will higher education reshape itself to go about the business of research and education in new ways? By raising such questions, we have narrowed the discussion of consortia to a few central issues, each of which is significant to the future of our industrial enterprises and educational system.

We then identify four categories of choices to be made by those engaged in creating and running consortia in *Part III*: "Partners," "Money & Influence," "The Agenda," and "Leadership." Each is illustrated with examples taken from our case studies. Together they explain the range and complexity of choices that go into constructing a consortium effort. They help explain why no two are alike.

Part IV focuses on a single consortium. We call it "The MCC: Doing It Texas Style." It describes the workings of an important and unique group in Austin, Texas, the Microelectronics and Computer Technology Corporation. Supporters see it as America's most significant private R&D initiative. Critics argue that despite its lavish funding it is ill crafted to make a dent on the competitive position of its sponsors. Either way, the MCC is under the gun to show results.

Finally, *Part V* concludes with a "What If..." chapter that explores possible outcomes of these initiatives. All of this is appended by descriptive facts and figures on the fourteen consortia and copies of two legal documents defining partners' rights in two consortia—one at Carnegie-Mellon University, the other at Stanford University. Each illustrates ways in which partner rights and commitments were defined.

Authors' note: The following sources may be of interest to the reader.

Botkin, J.; D. Dimancescu; and R. Stata. *Global Stakes: The Future of High Technology in America*. Cambridge, Mass.: Ballinger Publishing Co., 1982; paperback New York: Viking Penguin, 1984.

Botkin, J.; D. Dimancescu; and R. Stata. *The Innovators: Rediscovering America's Creative Energy*. New York: Harper and Row, 1984; paperback Philadelphia: University of Pennsylvania Press, 1986.

Fenwick, D., ed. *Directory of Campus-Business Linkages: Education and Business Prospering Together*. New York: American Council on Education/Macmillan, 1983.

Haklisch, C.; H. Fusfeld; and A. Levenson. *Trends in Collective Industrial Research*. New York: Center for Science and Technology Policy, New York University, 1984.

Haller, H. "Examples of University-Industry (Government) Collaborations." Office of the Vice President for Research & Advanced Studies, Cornell University. March 20, 1984. (Unpublished.)

Lynton, E. *The Missing Connection Between Business and the Universities*. New York: American Council on Education/Macmillan, New York, 1983.

National Research Council. *The New Engineering Research Centers: Purposes, Goals, and Expectations*. Washington, D.C.: National Research Council, 1986.

Newman, F. *Higher Education and the American Resurgence*. Princeton, N.J.: Carnegie Corporation for the Advancement of Teaching, 1985.

Peters, L., and H. Fusfeld. *University-Industry Research Relationships*. Washington, D.C.: National Science Foundation, 1982.

Part I
CONSORTIA

Chapter 1

THE EXPERIMENT

A small town in northern New England is an unlikely place to start a discussion about R&D consortia. Yet on a cold, wintery day in 1986, one of the co-authors drove along two-lane winding roads to reach a small New Hampshire town. Keene is home to the Kingsbury Machine Tool Corporation, a management-owned company run by James Koontz, its president.

At a time when machine tool companies are dying as fast as high-tech companies are starting up—there were 1,200 machine tool companies in 1981 and only 400 left in 1985—Kingsbury is an exception. With a worldwide work force of about 1,100, it is thriving largely as a result of wise management and an ability to absorb advanced technology into a new generation of machine-tool and flexible manufacturing systems.

Another reason for this company's success is James Koontz. A forceful spokesman for an embattled industry, this has led him more and more frequently to Washington, D.C. In conjunction with the National Research Council's Commission on Engineering and Technical Systems, he chairs a committee that is designing a new consortium. Its goal is to marry the interests of machine-tool makers and users into a National Center for Manufacturing Sciences. A ten-year plan is proposed that would raise a $500 million endowment that in turn would help support an annual research and technology agenda at a rate of $20 to $50 million a year. These are big bucks and big ideas.

What's important in his effort is a realization, as James Koontz puts it, "that there is a great deal of research work going on that duplicates itself over and over in the manufacturing world. There needs to be a central place where much of this can be gathered and duplication avoided." There is in his initiative an equal concern that knowledge may be flowing too rapidly from U.S. research centers into the hands of foreign competitors. "We have to design a center that serves as many members—U.S. members—as possible. We want companies to be able to 'buy-in' cheaply and get the maximum out of it," he says. "We don't want to restrain the freedom of information flow but we do want to get a leg up on others by seeing developments in universities and laboratories before others do." James Koontz and his colleagues' concerns are widely shared in various industries throughout the United States. Consortia are an experiment in trying to reverse the tide.

What is a consortium? The dictionary defines it is "any association or partnership." In finance, the term was long used to label groupings formed to pool resources. A humorist might correctly add that a consortium is also defined as "a husband's right to the company, help, and affection of his wife, and the right of his wife to the same." While marital affection is not the subject of this book, the shared relations between three social institutions—industry, government and academe—are.

We use the term *consortium* to define partnerships of universities or nonprofit research institutes with at least two or (usually) more companies—and on many occasions government agencies (federal, state, or local)—banded together to fund research and development. Notably absent are labor unions. Our focus of inquiry is on the interrelationships that develop among industry, academic enterprises, and governments or other third parties such as foundations.

For convenience, though not strictly accurate, we can classify consortia into three groups. One is the pre-1970 relationships including industrial affiliates programs or industry association efforts that were generally small in size—in the $1 to $5 million range—and with limited scope—for example contract research on tobacco growing techniques.

A second group are three special cases of regulated industries: the gas association, the electricity association, and the new communications association, Bellcore, formed from the seven regional operating companies formerly of AT&T. These are giant groupings with budgets ranging from $100 million to nearly $1 billion.

The third group is the focus of our attention and at the heart of the new debates. These are the accelerating number of industry-university consortia that began around 1980, although some started earlier and others were founded a few years later. These tend to range considerably in size, from under $1 million to more than $100 million, but for the most part they are considerably larger than their earlier counterparts. They tend to be in the $5 to $50 million range, and focus on knowledge-intensive technologies such as information technology, semiconductors, robotics, telecommunications, optics, medical and agricultural biotechnologies, or advanced materials like ceramics and polymers.

These consortia are different from their predecessors. Most of the more recent ones, formed during the 1980s, have come in response to the challenges of international competitors—*survival* and *threat* are words commonly heard echoing in the laboratories where industry-university consortia are housed. Most of the new consortia focus on high technology and on educating a new generation of technologists. And many are a direct result of antitrust laws first relaxed late in Jimmy Carter's presidential administration. In 1984, this relaxation was formalized further in amendments to the National Cooperative Research Act. Between 1984 and 1985 alone, forty-five new or proposed consortia were created, according to the U.S. Department of Commerce.

If their importance were measured purely in dollars, their impact would appear modest at best. The combined new consortia, if one excludes the deregulated phone companies' mammoth Bellcore, spend less than $300 million a year. The fourteen leading consortia we studied together spent no more than $200 million in 1986. Matched against a national R&D budget of almost $117 billion—civilian and defense—the sum seems inconsequential. Yet, one way to think of this seemingly meager infusion of funds is as ''money on the margin.'' This, like the athlete who comes rested off the bench at a critical moment, may just be the margin that makes the difference. Therefore, it is as an experiment in redefining the

5

nation's sense of economic mission by forging new partnerships that the impact of these new consortia must be evaluated.

What Would It Take?

The national economy is pressured by new forces of change. Some are global, induced by new competitors. Others are technological, as research yields the potential for better products and processes. Some are structural, as new industries displace older ones. While much of this had become apparent starting in the early 1970s, it took almost a decade for many Americans to accept the reality of the United States rapidly losing its competitive edge in world markets.

Those promoting the creation of consortia understood that our institutions—government, business, and academe—would have to change if the economy were to regain its momentum. "Consortia," says Dr. George Pake, vice president for research and development at Xerox, "are a response to a new concept of turning ideas into wealth." In practice, this meant that universities would have to reevaluate research agendas that are often removed from the economic mainstream; government would have to go beyond being a "wait and see" promoter of the public interest or a "guns-at-any-cost" spender of the public wealth; industry would have to forego a "go-it-alone" approach and would have to reconsider pooling resources with unlikely partners.

President Richard Cyert of Carnegie-Mellon University sees a joining of industry and university cooperation as one of America's greatest comparative advantages. "There's no place in the world where you have it this way. But we haven't had it to the extent we should or could have. Many in business finally recognize that it is brainpower—not manpower—that we must compete in." In Pittsburgh, this joining of forces illustrated by Carnegie-Mellon's Robotics Institute has led to a rejuvenation of the regional economy. Steel is the past, fueled by coal; electronically driven industries are the future, fueled by software.

The times call for a renewed effort to accelerate the nation's rate of economic growth. A century ago, similar pressures resulted in the creation of land grant colleges. During the 1850s, at that time in the context of populism, there was a desire to focus American higher education more on real problems. This contrasted sharply with an intellectually elitist and tightly hierarchical European counterpart.

The response, after years of deferment in the U.S. Congress, was the passage of the Morrill Act in 1862, which created the land grant college system. Many of these are now leading state universities, such as the University of Michigan or the University of California, and private ones such as MIT, which is still-a land grant college. Cornell, likewise, is referred to as half-private, half public, because several of its schools are still supported from public land grant funds.

Those colleges and universities, created by the federal government with the lure of land donations to states, broke with the past by denying a formula for high education founded on mastering the classics. Instead, they argued, and eventually proved, the value and viability of an education system focused on the "mechanical and agricultural arts." In today's language we would call it engineering and technology. It was clear, too, to the originators of these institutions that the liberal arts could, and should, remain central components of the curriculum.

During the post-World War II period higher education institutions, including the land grants, diverged from this mission. Many universities diversified their offerings and grew to enormous size. In many cases they spurred the expansion of pure science and research environments with funds provided with largesse by the federal government. Size and complexity bred bureaucracies and the attendant inertia. In many cases, the technology mission not only got lost but was consciously held in disdain. "If it's hands on, it can't be scholarship or science," went the criticism. But that was during the 1950s and 1960s when America's economic prominence went largely unchallenged worldwide. Not so in the 1970s or 1980s. Our productivity is down and our competitive advantages are eroded. Economic challengers abound.

"What would it really take to make an impact on America's industrial competitiveness?" asks Professor John Linvill, co-director of Stanford University's Center for Integrated Systems. "We've got to remember the magnitude of the post-World War II investment in graduate universities. It changed the course of engineering and research programs." In reference to a rapid rise in numbers of R&D consortia during the 1980s, he adds: "The ones that succeed will be important beyond our highest expectations. That's a very important thing for the American public to know."

Some leaders in academic institutions have understood the need to shift institutional missions to more explicit economic goals. In 1985, at the University of Massachusetts-Amherst, Joseph Duffey, its chancellor, stated in his annual report: "The challenge to our economy is clear, and the University of Massachusetts at Amherst has a role to play in it. . . . As our national economy becomes more dependent upon new technologies and knowledge-based industries, the importance of our University in [the partnership of government, education and business] must surely increase." Consortia manifest the realization of such ambitions.

Three Consortia

One example is the Semiconductor Research Corporation. Located in the wing of a low-rise commercial building at Research Triangle Park in North Carolina, its offices may be unimposing. But its origins and operations are quite the opposite. To the surprise of many, its creation was crafted by IBM, a company thought to be well protected from foreign competition. "Not only has the U.S. research effort been decreasing during the last few years," said Erich Bloch, an IBM senior executive and SRC co-founder in 1982 and now director of the National Science Foundation, "but costs of doing research have been escalating."[*]

In effect IBM had come to recognize that even it, too, could not go it alone against the Japanese. This came at a time when the federal government was apparently losing interest in funding pure research of the kind that had been so successfully promulgated during the NASA years. It was also recognized that many of the nation's leading academic research centers had lost touch with industry. "The SRC," said Bloch, "will assist . . . by investing the major portion of the research funds in universities and not-for-profit institutes, thereby funding new research positions and attracting new talent to these endeavors."

The SRC, a collaborative of twenty U.S. companies, was both an outcome of the changing rules of the game, meaning relaxed antitrust pressures, as well as a changer of the rules. By 1985, the effects were dramatic. Whereas three years before, public support for pure research for

[*]Bloch made this quote prior to being named NSF director. See *Global Stakes*, p. 183.

semiconductors was largely a federal matter involving about $7 million a year, industry now outpaced it by nearly three to one. By 1985, the SRC was investing about $20 million a year in *pure* research. These funds supported the work of almost 500 faculty and graduate students in forty universities. In short, industry was now determining the principal national agenda in semiconductors.

SRC efforts sought to restore competitive strength to the commercial makers of semiconductors, a goal increasingly overlooked by the federal government and overdue in a number of the nation's leading research universities. For the moment, however, Japanese producers continue to succeed in capturing rising shares of commercial markets for semiconductors because of production line innovations. As a result, for U.S. producers much of the pressure is on making their production processes more efficient. Management technology may be more vital to them than new product technology. In this regard, the SRC's successes could easily go underutilized if its members cannot themselves improve their management practices.

Another example of an experimental partnership is the Microelectronics Center of North Carolina (MCNC). Founded by the state government with a goal of stimulating economic development, five universities and the Research Triangle Institute are partners. Four companies joined early on, including GE, which located a $100 million plant near the Center. Later, four more joined. Housed in a sleek-looking complex, the consortium coordinates the work of 150 faculty and staff and about 200 university-based associates. All are focused on submicron silicon chip technologies backed by more than $80 million in mostly public capital investments. Part of it helped finance a state-of-the-art silicon semiconductor fabrication laboratory.

One of the Center's achievements is in bringing individuals face-to-face who might otherwise rarely cross paths. "There's a cooperative dialogue going on here with government and universities," says James Dykes, vice president and general manager of GE's Semiconductor Division, "which none of us had ever seen before." In many ways, just the fact of this dialogue fulfills many of the "highest expectations" expressed by Professor John Linvill. Indeed, the Microelectronics Center of North Carolina has far exceeded the expectations of all involved in its creation. Originally conceived as a regional research activity, it is now recognized worldwide as a leader in the field. Its activities have helped attract large firms to Research Triangle Park and have strengthened university resources substantially in the state.

A third example, perhaps the most complex administrative combination we studied, is Rensselaer Polytechnic Institute's (RPI) Center for Industrial Innovation. It encompasses three preexisting RPI centers with a thicket of names and initials: the Center for Manufacturing Productivity (CMP founded in 1979), the Center for Interactive Computer Graphics (CIG founded in 1978), and the Integrated Electronics Center (IEC founded in 1980). Each of these centers in their own right qualifies as a major industry-university consortium. The CIG alone has thirty-eight industrial partners, and is considered the top graphics laboratory in the world. (See Appendix B for an illustrative list of state-of-the-art equipment.)

What got them started? Graham Jones, director of the New York State Science and Technology Foundation, says that "it was the high tech/ Japan challenge that got them going." The three centers were brought under one unit in 1982 with the award of an interest-free loan from New York State of $30 million, matched by another $30 million from the school, to construct a building that integrates the activities of all three centers.

One of them is the Center for Manufacturing Productivity and Technology Transfer (CMP). Its activities are divided into two main types of activities: projects and programs. Projects are short, six- to fifteen-month research contracts signed with individual companies to produce a specific product. There are sixteen companies with eighteen contracts at approximately $150,000 each. Corporate participants include such names as NA Philips, Timex, Allied Technologies, Cincinnati Milacron, Boeing, Fairchild, GM, Schlumberger, and Hughes Aircraft. But if the CMP is itself a consortium within a consortium, it houses its own third-tier consortium.

Within the CMP is the CIM (Computer-Integrated Manufacturing) program funded for three years by seven corporations (IBM, DEC, Alcoa, GE, Kodak, Norton, and United Technologies) at a level of $7 million. From the CIM spill a chain of acronyms. Together they represent the full integration of CAD (Computer-Aided Design) with CAE (Computer-Aided Engineering), CAT (Computer-Aided Testing), CAM (Computer-

Aided Manufacturing), and business planning. The RPI school of management is a participant in the CIM consortium. Projects are organized by workteams: a project manager, faculty, industry engineers, and students. CIM is considered by Digital Equipment Corporation's vice president Ron Cadieux to be the finest program of its kind in the country. It illustrates the interdisciplinary linkages that can be created within seemingly conventional academic walls.

Rearranging the Pieces

What's happening? What are these consortia crafting? Dr. Terry Loucks is an executive with the newly created title of vice president of corporate technology at Norton Company, a rapidly changing old-line abrasives company in Worcester, Massachusetts. He says:

> After Sputnik and Apollo, a post-war peak, we saw the demise of strong central corporate R&D labs. They were shed as overly expensive technology resources. They lost communication with universities. But now with new technologies offering new solutions where do you turn? To government labs? They haven't been very cooperative, at least to date. So, it was back to the academics, and lo and behold we found they hadn't given up. They were still amazingly strong. Things weren't always in the right piles. But people began to rearrange academia to make it more useful to meeting the national [economic] threat.

"The thing that has drawn industry and universities together," states John Wilson, manager of planning for corporate R&D at Cincinnati Milacron, "is joint survival in the technology area. We're saying our success as a company is going to depend on our relationship with a university."

The implications for his company's future are dire, indeed. Its sales plummeted from a near high of $1 billion in 1981 to a pauce $660 million two years later and lower again in 1986. The situation is not unfamiliar to academic institutions faced with equipment shortages, lack of funds for faculty salaries, and new building needs. Survival is very much the new business of the 1980s. In this light, consortia are a vital experiment in pooling limited resources and institutionalizing common interests.

"What's important," says Frank Newman, president of the Education Commission of the States and past president of the University of Rhode

Island, "is that there is a climate created within which there is enough knowledge and above all a certain spirit by which things get done. The consortia—indeed many industry and university relationships—should create points of sharing knowledge as well as an innovative spirit that includes sharing of people," he argues.

It is important to keep in perspective, then, that these new consortia are still experimental. No one can foretell how long they will last, whether or not they are harbingers for the future, whether they are a pattern that we will watch expand and multiply hundreds of times, or whether in a decade or two they will atrophy. But even at this experimental stage, the payoff seems sure to be big.

Project Athena, one of the fourteen consortia we studied, is such an experiment. Professor Joel Moses, head of MIT's electrical engineering and computer sciences department, pointed out: "All of Athena is a grand experiment. If we're not surprised by something in the end then it wasn't a very interesting experiment." But Athena promises a lot, as Moses states:

> We are really trying to accelerate some of the learning that comes from experience. We will have to do the same experiments, but it might not take as long, and the makework will be eliminated. It might be possible to do simulated chemical experiments prior to going in to get your hands on the beakers. A further way to learn to anticipate outcomes and get an intuitive feel.

> There are many people in engineering from the older generation that have done so many equations and problems in a particular field that they have an intuitive sense. In the transition from the slide rule to the calculator the art of estimation was lost to the science of the digital chip. Perhaps with Athena we can reinvent something that we've lost.

Such comments highlight a significant feature of R&D consortia. They are propelling universities into the fore as active partners in stimulating economic development. This sense of mission, familiar to some institutions such as MIT, Stanford, and more recently Carnegie-Mellon, had either lapsed in many others or was never apparent. This is surprising, given the roots of so many colleges that were born out of the land grant traditions of the prior century. Are we perhaps returning to the uniquely American tradition of the university as a center of technology? Does the forming of consortia portend a shift in the university's sense of mission?

Is technology—or the art of giving commercial utility to knowledge—not only in vogue but also a necessary focus of the academic enterprise? When we decided to look more deeply into the phenomenon of R&D consortia, such questions guided our curiosity.

Chapter 2

NEW ATTITUDES

So what's new to be gleaned from the new consortia, and what's all the fuss or fervor about? What's new, above all, is a change in *attitude* within universities, industry, and government. A sense of common interest is taking root of a kind that hasn't existed before. What's more significant is that substantial resources, reputations, and political collateral are being put at risk in turning these new attitudes into tangible form.

Some, and some of our most prestigious, universities are seeking industrial relationships and ties that go far beyond simple charitable fundraising. Stanford's Center for Integrated Systems has signed up 20 companies, Rutgers ceramics center counts 31, Carnegie-Mellon's Robotics Center has about 28, the Microelectronics and Computer Technology Corporation (better known as the MCC), loosely affiliated with the University of Texas in Austin and Texas A&M, has 21. RPI has 58 partners. This is big business, and some wonder whether this should indeed be the business of the university—assuming, incorrectly perhaps, that universities have indeed a single business or mission.

At the same time, companies are seeking out universities, and this represents another change of attitude. Having retreated from many campuses during the post-World War II period, the situation is reversed. Digital and IBM initially battled one another to help MIT—both are now giving money, equipment, and personnel to the tune of $50 million to MIT alone. Digital itself, only one-tenth IBM's size, is a participant in more than twenty university ventures—not just to sell equipment or influence future buyers, although this too may be part of the motivation. The key goal is innovation—developing new products and processes—and access to the rarest commodity—the brainpower of talented human resources.

Not surprisingly, state governments, too, have undergone a change of attitude—at least a good dozen of them. The State of New York, for example, has a well-conceived, well-funded, and to date well-executed strategy for creating high-tech industry-university "centers of advanced technology" (CATs). So do New Jersey, Michigan, Indiana, and Pennsylvania, among others, have coherent strategies. North Carolina's initiative, sparked some twenty-five years ago, is a successful, oft-cited model that many would emulate if they only could.

Paradoxically, some states, like Massachusetts and California, have less well-developed programs—some would say they were slow to the mark, or off of it altogether, perhaps because they had a head start on everyone, much of it fueled early on by heavy investments of federal defense dollars and later by homegrown venture capital funds. Until recently, some states like Illinois have been surprisingly slow to act. But one thing is clear. Most state governments are aware of the job-creating, tax-base-enhancing potential of this new phenomenon, the industry-university consortium, and they have jumped on the bandwagon.

A distinct shift has occurred. Naturally, not all universities have responded to the change, nor need they do so. One of the strengths of the American educational system is its sheer diversity. We can afford to bet on different combinations of liberal arts, industrial programs, and government research and discover by trial, error, and intelligent choice which ones work, which ones make sense for our times.

But the tendency is in a specific direction. Frank Newman states:

> When I was at Stanford, I was struck by the fact that we were always prepared to discuss issues of technology whereas Berkeley—the state university—would never do that. Berkeley's now changing a lot of that. At Stanford more departments are willing to get in and actually talk with industry. Yale is like the old Berkeley—staunchly sticking to liberal arts with a disdain for applied technology. On the horizon, I think that there will be more Stanfords and fewer Yales. In ten years, whereas there are 10-12

Stanfords and 100 Yales today, there will be 70 to 80 Stanfords and the rest of them Yales.

What's behind this "more Stanfords, less Yales" move? What drives the new marriage between industry and university, or the new menage a trois if state or federal goverment is playing a role, which is more often than not the case? Part of it is that the luxury of costly pure research labs with uncertain outcomes is under fire. One reason is simply the reality of the economic challenge from abroad.

Global Competition

It was during the 1970s that the United States' economic vitality came into question. With the rapid rise of Japan as an industrial peer and a lackluster performance by a number of key U.S. industries, Americans looked for new ways of reviving the economic tempo. Increasingly during the late 1970s and early 1980s, industry turned to universities and colleges as a source of ideas and people to fuel its growth needs.

Technology has always been seen as a source of economic strength for the U.S. economy. Even when Japan's Ministry of International Trade and Industry (MITI) declared in 1980 the nation's intention of becoming the world's leading innovator and technological power, few Americans took it seriously. As late as 1982, we were still running a healthy trade surplus with Japan, not in autos and manufactured products but in agriculture and most importantly, high-tech products. By 1984, those numbers for high technology had dramatically reversed. That year, much to our consternation, figures showed Japan exporting five times as much technology to the United States as we sold to it. In overall world trade, U.S. high-technology exports fell from a massive $8 billion surplus in 1980 to an alarming $8 billion deficit in 1984. Semiconductors fell from a positive $500 million to a minus $3 billion during the same period. By 1985, our overall deficit with Japan in all trade was $50 billion or about one-third the total national trade deficit. One reason for the drop was explained by currency exchange rates. But the real answer was in the growing technological strength of countries like Japan.

While global competition may have sparked the creation of the consortia we studied, it also presents its own dilemma—namely that knowledge like money or grain is fungible. It ignores barriers, and it travels swiftly from one country to another. While many American educators and policy-makers emphasize the national benefits of consortia, many U.S. businesses are world enterprises unfettered by the concept of national boundaries.

Such global relationships are not uncommon to U.S. industry. Emhart Corporation in Connecticut helped stimulate the creation of an international glassmakers consortia that came together in 1984. It combines resources from firms in the United States, Japan, Australia, the United Kingdom, and West Germany. In other cases, firms enter into extensive technology transfer co-ventures, as AT&T did in 1983 when it joined forces with Lucky-Goldstar, a large South Korean conglomerate. IBM has numerous links worldwide.

But if companies themselves are part of the reason technology moves across national boundaries so fast, so is the nature of American university admission policies. Their very openness to all-comers—a feature that we are not recommending be changed—means that a huge number of foreign students, many on leave from corporations, are enrolled. In engineering Ph.D. programs, the number of foreign students has surpassed American ones. Although there is the beneficial by-product of new talent coming to the United States and potentially staying on, there is also the dilemma of students returning home loaded down with the latest technological know-how. Some observers believe that Japan—and other countries—has tapped this open academic resource extensively and much to their advantage without returning equivalent knowledge. An example is NEC, a Japanese electronics giant. It sends an annual delegation to MIT to roam the laboratories in search of new ideas, faculty contacts, and students. The firm's chairman, an MIT graduate, frequently leads the way walking the halls with an entourage of assistants taking notes in preparation for further contact with faculty and students. American corporate CEOs ought to take a lesson here and start cultivating Japanese centers of research.

Within consortia, generally open attitudes toward knowledge-flow change when it comes to Japan. Most are reluctant about, or even adamantly against, Japanese participation. None of the consortia we studied had Japanese members. There was an underlying concern that the Japanese strategy might be simply to watch and wait for the results of American industry-university consortia.

"We won't even talk to Japanese companies," says Christopher W. LeMaistre, himself an Australian who is director of Rensselaer Polytechnic Institute's George M. Low Center for Industrial Innovation. "They listen and observe but never give anything in return. I know Mitsubishi would give us $1 million dollars, but so far we have refused."

But knowledge and know-how travel easily. They do not stick to a formal path and the dilemma of beating the Japanese—or others—to the punch may still be unresolved in spite of the closed membership groundrule of most consortia. For the present, the issue may better be cast as a matter of pace than possession. Time measured in months rather than years can often mean the difference in getting a lead on a competitor. Staying ahead with new ideas may be what the new alliance provides. But is new technology and its implicit knowledge intensity really where the game can be won?

New Technologies

What do we mean by *high technology*? Knowledge-intensive investment in a product or service is one defining characteristic; the high cost of generating it is another. In practice, the description we use is straightforward: A high-tech industry is one in which a very high proportion of employees are trained in technical, engineering, or scientific skills. Alternatively, one might use a companion characteristic that high-tech industries are those that spend a high proportion of sales dollars on research. This can range from 5 to 15 percent in high-tech firms. The employment characteristic is more telling, however, because it says something about the educational component of this industry. In electronics, for example, a high-tech enterprise will have a workforce with 20 to 30 percent of its employees having B.S. degrees or better (mostly in electrical engineering and computer science); another 30 percent will have technical education; the balance will be trained in non-technical fields or be unskilled. By these measures about 3 to 6 percent of the U.S. workforce is currently employed in high-tech firms. Projections to the end of the century do not show a dramatic increase in that proportion.

The high-tech employment profile, with its stress on highly qualified personnel, underscores the importance of knowledge as a strategic competitive ingredient. Preparing a critical mass of students, or upgrading current workers, to excel in high-tech industries is not just essential, it will be the central determinant of economic vitality for a given region, state, or nation. It is the starting point from which to build a vibrant economic base in the coming decades. That is why universities have a central role to play. This function, recognized by the advent of consortia and reinforced by the newly instituted National Science Foundation's Engineering Research Centers program, is generally misunderstood by the general public as an issue of major national importance.

One effect is an underfunding of higher education. The outcome is a shortage of skilled people not just in the narrow sense of technical specialization but also in the broader sense of being adept at understanding global issues and a global marketplace. In the technical fields, a major problem is limited university capacity and a consequent undermining of teaching and research quality. Two-thirds of the country's accredited engineering departments have capped or reduced engineering enrollments. In more than two dozen of them, accreditation is being challenged because of overcrowding. In many others, qualified students are turned away. At the University of California at Berkeley, there were 3,786 qualified engineering applicants for 525 positions in the undergraduate class of 1982; by 1985 there were only 9 new openings in the class of 1985 or a total of 534. At Purdue University, the average class size in engineering doubled between 1971 and 1982 before a cap was put on enrollments. A cap is still on. At the University of Texas (UT) in Austin, during the same period, undergraduate engineering was reduced from 6,500 to 5,800 and graduate enrollment limited to 1,350. Overall enrollment has fallen further to 5,042 in 1985, although at the graduate level there's been an increase to 1,507. The UT electrical engineering department is "overextended" according to administrators, and limits have been set. In oil states such as Texas, declining oil prices' have exacerbated the problem.

The point is that the nation's engineering departments are facing a *capacity crunch* resulting in part from a drain of graduate and teaching staff into industry and by an inadequate supply of funds for equipment and facilities. This capacity problem can be solved by a judicious infusion of funds—which have traditionally been available from public sources (state and federal). New partnerships between industry, academia, and government are part of the solution. Will universities lead in seeking them out?

20

engineering or science curricula to other disciplines are another part of the solution. Who will push to see that this is achieved and financed?

Push or Pull?

Lively debate will ensue from a discussion of whether technological ideas get pushed into the marketplace from the laboratory, or, whether marketplace demands pull them out of the lab. In Japan, this subject is often described as a mediation between *seeds* and *needs*. The former are ideas that emanate from open-ended laboratory research; the latter are specific demands imposed on the firm by the marketplace. Do too much of the first and you'll lose marketshare; do too much of the latter and you'll lose market leadership. The well-managed firm or economy, say the Japanese, is the one that finds the optimal interface between the two. This is normally done within the firm by management teams, but it is also a process of mediation engaged in by MITI at the national industrial level.

The American corporate dilemma is that it is hasn't optimized the seeds/needs relationship. In many enterprises old habits and hierarchical structures are inhibiting the movements of ideas, especially when it comes to letting marketplace desires flow upstream toward corporate decision-makers. This means lost time in getting ideas translated into products. Often it means lost opportunity. In most cases, we are far better at nurturing the seeds or R&D side. During the post-World War II federal priorities helped shift much of the basic research responsibility to the university. In some industries such as pharmaceuticals, companies literally gave up on basic research and spent most of their R&D dollars on testing drugs. One effect is that the needs side is often left unattended and basic research veers off in unrelated directions. The quality of work being done may be high and respected, but its contribution to strengthening our competitive advantage in world markets becomes more and more tenuous. One contribution of consortia may be in providing a better mechanism to mediate the seeds/needs relationship by bringing university and indus-try—frequently with government involvement—together in determining the joint research agenda. What was a *push* of ideas out of labs into the market is being redefined by consortia as a marketplace *pull* of ideas. The consequences are not unimportant to the future competitiveness of the economy.

consequences are not unimportant to the future competitiveness of the economy.

One of the first joint-research co-ventures was pioneered by a professor of chemistry at the University of Kansas in 1906, when Robert Duncan brought to the United States an idea already in practice in Europe. This caught the attention of the University of Pittsburgh, which invited him, in 1910, to start a special institute. Its job would be to link the academic enterprise to industry. Out of this was born the Mellon Institute three years later—and with it a unique form of industry fellowships. This idea of interchange between corporate and university laboratories became institutionalized with the now-widespread industrial affiliates programs, many of which thrive in numerous universities to this day.

Another innovation occurred during the 1920s and 1930s with the birth of ventures like the Electrical Power Institute or the Tobacco Institute, where industries worked with universities on a variety of research topics. And, of course, the agriculture/academia connection dates back to the 1862 Morrill Act, which resulted in the land grant university system and agricultural extension stations that brought state and federal governments into partnership with the farming industry.

This brings up the whole issue of whether the time is not ripe for a major revolution in the educational equivalent to the 1860s when the Morrill Act was passed creating the land grant college system. "Absolutely!" says Linvill.

We are, of course, aware of how difficult such a change in thinking is to achieve. "May I remind you that the academic community—almost to a person—opposed the Morrill Act," says Frank Newman, himself a former president of a land grant university:

> It transformed the universities. We eventually became research universities as a result of that set of initiatives. Yet, it was opposed. An attempt was made to subvert it. Brown University in Rhode Island, Yale in Connecticut, became land-grant institutions. They soon lost it. That's because they were trying to subvert it. A lot of private colleges subverted it. Only two private ones are left: MIT and Cornell. Basically what happened was that new institutions were created and we subverted the university process.

Professor John Linvill continues:

How would you have felt at the end of World War II when the Office of Naval Research had just done such an amazing job and the NSF was just set up? How would this influence the role of graduate education in the United States in the 1960s—you would have been pretty pessimistic. Yet it happened in spite of itself. In my opinion, these are experimental grounds at the moment and they have to be successful on their own turf. But if we do not have within a decade the same magnitude of effect on the way industry performs and the way education performs in both the technology and organization, then we've missed our opportunity.

Part II
FRAMING THE QUESTIONS

Chapter 3

CONTROL

Industry-university consortia may be the needed response to competitive challenges that, with some growth in size or numbers, would be commensurate to the threat. But if "we convey that by setting up these kinds of organizations nothing else in the institutions or the university has to change," says Marc Tucker, director of the Carnegie Forum in Washington, D.C., "then we are providing a disservice. In fact, one way to look at industry-university consortia is to see them as *impedance managers*. That is, are they an intermediary institution which allows the other larger ones—the university or industries—to resist or forgo fundamental change?"

Yet implicit in the consortia we studied are three kinds of changes. The first has to do with control of the research agenda, which is discussed in this chapter. The second has to do with making the transfer of technology process more effective and economically productive. The third has to do with institutional change and whether consortia will either defer that change or accelerate it. We consider these latter two in subsequent chapters.

Formally defined, *technology* is the application of science, especially to industrial or commercial objectives. But knowing what it means is quite different from knowing who determines the application or the ultimate objective. Just by asking the question "who sets the research agenda?" you quickly get to the bottom line of control.

Is it the university, is it industry, or is it government? Is the university's mission being undermined, as some claim, if others participate in setting the agenda? "Just because something is high tech doesn't mean it is good tech," said Terry A. Matilsky, an associate professor of physics at the New Jersey Center for Ceramics Research. "Corporate research needs will inevitably impinge on the freedom of academic researchers." Similarly, industry people might be prone to respond "just because it's university tech doesn't mean it's useful tech."

Perhaps the first question to be asked from a national perspective is "What kind of research do we want?" Do we want more pure research, a step removed from applied research? Do we want more development? Answering the question with numbers can be misleading. One could be quite impressed, for example, to note that of America's total expenditure of $117 billion on R&D in 1985, $57 billion was accounted for by the federal government. On closer analysis, the specifics—and the implied question of control—shed a different light. Almost $30 billion of the federal government's expenditures are defense related. And of that sum a massive 97 percent was allocated to weapons *development* programs. A pauce 3 percent went to *pure research*. One effect of such shifts in priority is not only to stress the use of existing technologies but to overwhelm the agenda with defense applications. The effect is to reduce our overall investment in civilian R&D to rates that now put us well below Japan and West Germany.

Another reason for concern is that post-war experience shows that huge basic research programs such as NASA, the Atomic Energy Commission, and defense have been notoriously unproductive in producing commercially attractive technologies. This view is argued strongly by Professor Gerhard Mensch of the University of Berlin, a respected authority on technology and innovation. Of these programs he says, "very few attempts to push these new technologies in the civilian sector have made any significant impact on the economy."[*] He calls this the "paradox of technologies:" abundant new knowledge sitting unused.

The business of control becomes significant when one considers the "national security" constraints associated with defense-related research. Federal contracts are more and more accompanied by strict requirements

[*]Gerhard Mensch, *Stalemate in Technology* (Cambridge, Mass.: Ballinger Publishing Co., 1979) p. 155.

that research be engaged in a closed shop. This is hardly the setting required to stimulate a flow of knowledge into the civilian sector. For some programs like the Defense Advanced Research Projects Agency's (known as DARPA and also as ARPA) Information Processing Technologies Office (IPTO), which has been exceptionally effective in stimulating civilian technology for more than two decades, the implications are severe. IPTO has been the principal funder of computer science research in U.S. universities. With the coming of the Strategic Defense Initiative (SDI) popularly know as "Star Wars," and an accelerated fear of technology flow to the Soviet Union, a tradition of openness in sharing research findings is quickly coming to an end.

For academics who have been primary recipients of federal research dollars a serious dilemma has ensued. Research dollars from nondefense sources have not risen significantly. This puts pressure on them to accept defense contracts at the price of losing control over the academic freedom normally associated with such research. The advent of the SDI agenda—and its lavish budget—has caused intense debate in academic circles. Many researchers have refused to accept SDI-related monies because of the constraints. One effect of this changing national agenda has been to push academics into a more rapid embrace of industry relationships—especially those that might make up for diminished pure research budgets. The attractiveness of consortia with large, pooled resources is a coveted option.

But consortia may not be interested in the same research agenda as that nurtured in prior years by federal programs. Once again, one encounters a two faceted question of control. One facet is the matter of substance. What is going to be the agenda when it is industry that pays the bills—or industry in partnership with a state or a foundation? The other facet is, at what price to academic freedom? Consortia arrangements straddle a line between openness by encouraging a free flow of information to all their members while restraining external flow of ideas as much as possible. It is this sort formula that James Koontz described in the opening paragraphs of the book. It is a dilemma with difficult resolution. Can one maximize information flow to as many *U.S.* members as possible and yet tightly control access to competing non-American firms—and not impinge on principles of academic freedom?

29

The ideal, of course, is that industry and university should jointly set an agenda, one that draws on the strengths of each party and preserves the rights and responsibilities of the other. Or if government is involved, particularly state government—which is common—that its role be passive. In practice, we were surprised to learn that in many cases industry is going the last mile to avoid dictating terms or timetables. "We expect the university to have the knowledge," says Terry Loucks at the Norton Company. "If they ask us what they should be doing, we're at the wrong university." In other cases, such as the Microelectronics Center of North Carolina (MCNC), the North Carolina state government has been assiduous and scrupulous in keeping at arm's-length from influencing the substance and implementation of the research agenda. Its interest is in seeing job growth as a by-product, which has been happening without its direct intrusion in the MCNC's affairs.

On another level, of course, the very existence of industry-university consortia implies that universities are doing work and working on an agenda of vital interest to companies. The University of Rochester and its Center for Advanced Optical Technology (CAOT) provides an interesting case study. To determine which projects to choose, its director, Kenneth Teegarden, selected six topics in consultation with the faculty. He did outline projects that he thought would be of interest to industry, but he did not consult his collaborating companies before selecting the projects. Its four founding members—Kodak, Corning, Xerox, and Bausch and Lomb—were happy to let the university bring its expertise to bear. One might almost say the companies exhibited an attitude of aloofness. Only Kodak to date has sent any researchers to work on the Rochester campus to participate directly in the research, let alone determine the research agenda.

The CAOT's coming into being demonstrates in part the activist role state government can play. "When New York state decided that optics was a key technology," says Teegarden, "we were obliged to get industry matching funds. The state gave us only six weeks to show substantial industry support. The president of the university got four sponsors to immediately commit $2.7 million over four years. It was a spontaneous crystallization of our past history." The university probably could have raised more money in industry, but at the time, it said to the state, "We will simply match what you give us." The state said they wouldn't mind if the university "over-matched," but "we are trying to put pressure on the state to increase its allocations," adds Teegarden.

One problem is that the Optics Institute has two different kinds of sponsors. There are the original four founding sponsors who gave money with no conditions attached. "The CEOs simply signed pledges," recalls Teegarden. "Now my job is to get the additional money needed." The university needs to increase the original industry support by $1.3 million for a total of $4 million. But the second set of sponsors is less aloof. GE and IBM are two examples. They give money for one year at a time, and they want a specific contract of what they are going to get for their money.

"We are also haggling over patent rights," says Teegarden. "The first sponsors immediately assigned any patent rights to the university. But IBM is bargaining and insisting they want patent rights." In other words, the new sponsors, unlike the original four, want close control over the project and its evolution.

A different situation exists in parts of Rensselaer Polytechnic Institute's (RPI) program. Mary Johnson, manager of corporate relations at the Center for Interactive Computer Graphics at RPI, says "I write the contracts, and I'm the one who specifies the research program. Of course I take into account the wishes of the industrial sponsors, but they in no way dictate what we do. We set the agenda!" She says it with conviction, and her firmness is tough to challenge.

In nearly every case of the fourteen consortia we studied in detail, the issue of "openness" proved to be something of a red herring, over-stressed by those for whom any industrial relationship seemed threatening. True, in some cases, industry naively misjudged the importance of open dissemination of information, as happened early in the negotiations to create Stanford's CIS. But in most cases, we found that industry took extra steps to avoid impinging on university "rights." Terry Loucks, vice president of the Norton Company, says "We depend on the university for expertise. We neither want to set their agenda, which would be self-defeating, nor restrict the exchange of information among researchers."

Behind questions of who controls the agenda lies a deeper concern. These have to do with whether or not knowledge is transferred into the marketplace. For a long period the federal government stimulated economic development, it was believed, by spending massive amounts on basic research. But that was during post-war decades when foreign competition had yet to get on its feet. Today this relationship is no longer evident. As a result, we are led to reconsider the process of ''technology transfer.''

Chapter 4

TECHNOLOGY TRANSFER

Creation of technology alone is only half the process. The other half requires that it be moved into the economic mainstream. It may be, however, that as a nation we have worked much harder on the front end and far less on the uses of new technology. What's involved here is the transfer of new knowledge into commercially sound products or processes. But there are widely divergent concepts of what technology transfer means—and often misconceptions about how abstract or risk intensive the process is. Some see the process as moving real things from a loading dock to a customer. Others see it as a legal agreement that "licenses" a right to someone else. To others, it may be as extreme as a covert "stealing" of ideas. While to some, it is explained as an abstract endeavor without quantifiable characteristics.

We should be quick in stating that while there are no sure bets on how best to create new technology, there surely are no secret or easily replicable formulae on how best to transfer it into the marketplace. John Linvill, co-director of Stanford's Center for Integrated Systems (CIS), likes to note: "We mustn't fear failure too much. The magnitude of this as a problem is one in which you need to put a number of diversified bets down . . . and recognize that some of them are going to fail. From the ones that fail, at least you learn something."

33

The key point, we believe, is the one that relates to the *climate for innovation*. As Frank Newman states:

> In the process of talking about university-industry partnerships, there's a flaw in believing that we start with a deep idea in basic research which moves along from hand to hand to become an applied idea, then a developed idea, then a product that goes out the door. There are cases that sort of look like that. But that leaves no room for the flow in the opposite direction. The flawed view implies a very orderly movement—which we know from experience is not the case at all.
>
> Isn't it true that the most important role is something very different from what we've been looking for? We've been looking for vehicles for handling that relationship. Maybe what is more important is that there is a climate within which there is enough knowledge and most of all a certain spirit by which things get done. The industry-university relationship should create a point of sharing—knowledge, an innovative spirit, and a sharing of people and connection points. The electrical engineering affiliates program at Stanford was very informal but the climate allowed transfer both ways. Each does what it's good at and shares things in a way that makes a more exciting whole.

One view of technology transfer is that it moves with people. This produces a lively debate—the more so when the mover is an entrepreneur. Conflict arises between wanting to create technology, which means retaining creative people, and transferring it, which may mean losing them. Pat Crecine, academic vice president of Carnegie-Mellon University (CMU), has the unusual view that "the problem at CMU is the very success of consortia. In our case it's a robotics institute; artificial intelligence is the pure science and robotics the practical application. When you are successful at linking these pieces together," observes Crecine, "you attract the venture capitalists who go after the scarcest resource a university has—its intellectual capital of people. There is a lot of temptation to create spin-offs. The tension this creates in the institution is enormous. We'd like to follow up on benefits of doing a good job but not lose that vital resource. That's a very interesting challenge; in the long run, that's very fundamental."

A more visionary Silicon Valley response to this issue of talent raiding came from Professor John Linvill. "I agree that the situation exists. It's one of the concurrent conditions that comes along with success. We certainly want the most attractive people for the faculty who are also the most attractive to set up something on the outside. In general, I'm wondering whether that may not be the challenge the university needs to live with. We've got an enormous potential of new people coming through. And we make our problems of university attractiveness unnecessarily difficult by shellacking every new appointee with overdemands in terms of his publishing or perishing, with 'go out and get some support' for his research 'but we don't have any funds ourselves and you're awfully good at raising money.' And then hassling him about promotion and keeping his salary below what he's worth. So that's really the problem.

"We've got to do something about it," Linvill adds. "because we, like others, are losing people."

But there is another side, also, to this question of "transfer of technology." One misleading generalization is that the transfer is always from a university (the alleged fount of knowledge) to industry (the supposed users of technology). It is important, however, to realize that transfer is a *two-way street*. "I think that much to the university's chagrin or self image, more technology transfer will come to the university than will go to industry. That's a bad thing to say isn't it?" says Linvill half jokingly. "We strongly depend for new techniques and for forefront things upon a tight connection to our industrial sponsors and the people in the Stanford community. I'm telling you there is a two-way street. It's a corollary to the fact that the university and industry are each moving toward the other."

Was it "a bad thing to say?" No. The difference in the two-way streets is only how heavy the traffic flows in one direction versus another. MIT's Athena project, for example, has a heavy industry knowledge component flowing into the university to solve a university problem—how to build a workstation for under $10,000 that every student could use. Because of this focus, we often refer to the MIT case as a "reverse consortia." On the other hand, MIT is providing a huge amount of research and knowledge creation on the software side of the project. No fewer than twenty-five different parts of the Institute, from foreign languages to electrical engineering, are writing software programs of great interest and value to the industry—and raising issues once again about the ownership rights of these programs, an issue that we treat in more detail in Part III.

35

At the University of Rochester, there has been a major change in attitude about spin-offs as a legitimate faculty activity and the resulting technology transfer. Duncan T. Moore, an associate professor of optics, has started his own company and is rapidly transfering technology to his own firm.

"The most significant thing," he notes, "about the New York State involvement is that it has produced a favorable *change in attitude* toward faculty entrepreneurship. Since 1980—and 1980 is a good cut off date for this—faculty members have been encouraged to spawn new companies as a technology transfer mechanism. Before 1980 any faculty member who tried to start a new company met 'lots of grief'. It was discouraged. Now it's encouraged both by the state and the University of Rochester administration because of the CAT [Center for Advanced Technology]. New York State did not contribute to the development of technology but to the transfer of technology *via a change of attitude*."

The Cooked Noodle or Spaghetti Effect

"Technology is like a cooked noodle," says Frank Pitman of Carnegie-Mellon's Robotics Institute. This view mirrors ideas developed by Professor Mensch who writes: "The spaghetti effect explains the lack of innovations as the result of inertness of captains of industry. If you move one end of a limp piece of spaghetti, the other end will not move. A large fund of knowledge is building up, but it is affecting actual practice at a very slow rate. It is a well-established finding of innovation research that 'technology push' is an inferior way to introduce new technologies on the market; 'demand pull' is a major factor for successful innovation. If this demand is lacking, the rate of innovation is low." *

Numerous mechanisms have been created to accelerate or encourage the technology transfer process, but few models exists on how to do it best. Most of the R&D consortia we studied, and others we have followed, were created with technology transfer as a principal part of their agenda. But what technology transfer means to these fourteen consortia is far from uniform. Here are some examples.

*Gerhard Mensch, *Stalemate in Technology* (Cambridge, Mass.: Ballinger Publishing Co., 1979) p. 155

Jerry Schlensker, vice president of manufacturing at Cummins Engine, oversees his company's involvement in the Computer Integrated Design, Manufacturing and Automation Center (CIDMAC) at Purdue University. "At CIDMAC," he says, "the technical committee reviews ongoing work and transfers technology to the companies. For example, Cummins may get involved in a project focused on the product design process as part of the computer aided design portion. The technology committee will review it. Other companies can then choose to translate the work into their own terms by adding to or modifying the project."

Commenting on differences between CIDMAC at Purdue and the Robotics Institute at CMU for example, Schlensker added: "At CMU they provide the building and people; industry comes forward with a project. The project itself is the technology transfer. At Purdue the transfer is in generic research. The product or process comes later at the company." There, indeed, are two very different notions.

Don Beilman, president of the Microelectronics Center of North Carolina (MCNC), sees the process quite differently. "Companies take technology back through people here, not as a final product." This view is reinforced by James Dykes of GE Semiconductor who states: "With the exception of CAD software that might come out of MCNC, it's people we look for."

In Indiana, Alden McLellan, ex-president of the Corporation for Science and Technology (CST), had another view. "At CST we are mission oriented but not technology specific. Transfer of technology is the key. We want to see new ideas created and transferred. This has to be done through patents. CST keeps the licensing rights." Knowledge is held in the legally protected form of a patent and then "transferred" by selling it to a user in the marketplace.

In some cases, the process is described in vaguer terms. "Tech transfer, for us," says Professor Ted Kehl of the University of Washington/Northwest VLSI Consortium, "is knowledge transfer, pure and simple. A consortium can do it at low cost. Any one company could not do what we are doing alone."

At Stanford's Center for Integrated Systems (CIS), the Texas Instruments resident representative interpreted technology transfer as "seeing all that's going on and sending it back." One of his fellow representatives from GE saw the CIS as "the single point of contact to aid in transference of knowledge. There's a lot of good work in a university but it's spread out. The CIS consortium focuses the point of contact.'' Another form of knowledge transfer was explained by a representative from GTE who remarked that ''we can take clues about other corporate cultures back to his firm.''

Dr. Zvonko Faranzic, representing Hewlett Packard at the CIS, outlined his view on how technology transfer occurs: ''I maintain close contact with my research center and an informal relationship to HP's lab. I go there as a speaker. I attend seminars for sponsor reps. I direct the transfer of reports to HP. And I have direct meetings with my supervisor.''

Others saw technology transfer in a different light: ''Because of the way CIS works we are asking ourselves whether there are projects to be done here because of greater leverage and the resources. That question had never come up before. It's easier to capture expertise here.'' Reflecting on this range of views shared by industry reps over lunch one day, Professor Linvill said: ''You know something, we've never had this kind of contact before. Technology transfer—you know what it is? It's people.''

Between these contrasting views, if there is any sort of tacit agreement it is that technology transfer is something that cannot be left to chance. It needs to be ''managed.'' But what does proper management mean? Surprisingly, on this point there is little consensus, indeed little emphasis, in most of the collaborative projects we've been watching. Many of the consortia concentrate heavily on creating new technologies, few concentrate on how best to manage the transfer. This is a serious oversight—and in many cases the corporate partners (the users of the technologies) are largely to blame.

Where do management oversights occur? ''Company managers tend to underestimate the internal investment required to benefit from our work,'' says Raj Reddy who heads Carnegie-Mellon's Robotics Institute. ''There was a case with Westinghouse where we worked on a turbine blade problem. The managers involved weren't experienced with high tech. They weren't computer experts. The basics were foreign to them.'' Although the Robotics Institute demonstrated work stations that were networking controllers and doing parallel programming and space occupancy coordination, management couldn't tap the benefits. "These were all new issues to the company's turbine blade people," Reddy recalls.

And, there was the "intelligent scheduling" problem initially commissioned by Westinghouse at the Robotics Institute. "We saw that as a ten-year problem to solve. And Westinghouse turned it down. But we went on with it on our own. By year four we had a system demo," said Reddy. "But now for Westinghouse to use it, they'd have to invest a lot of time and energy. But they have no people. To succeed you need to be able to internalize new ideas and absorb them."

In most cases management isn't prepared to tackle the assignment or hasn't anticipated the internal cost involved. But to Professor Reddy, the balance sheet with Westinghouse has been more than favorable. Out of eight projects, one-half have led to technology transfer. "At least one of those was successful enough to pay the entire cost of all eight. That's a significant success to me."

Westinghouse is the Robotics Institute's biggest client. Many of the projects it funds are successfully implemented to everyone's satisfaction. The company has spent almost $5 million at the Robotics Institute over five years. "They've gotten a bang for their buck," says Raj Reddy. "It might have cost them ten times more to do the same things in-house."

Overall, the subject of managing new technology in the enterprise persists as a serious weakness of the R&D consortium movement. This offers an important clue, too, to a deeper weakness of the U.S. firms when it comes to competition against better managed Japanese firms. Thus, in this preliminary analysis of consortia, it became evident that none had deliberately set out to tackle the management of technology as a substantive concern.

With a couple of important exceptions, schools of management are not involved as partners in crafting technology development strategies. Their course material is weak or nonexistent when it comes to management of technology, and only occasionally does one find the engineer or technologist being consciously trained to be equally adept as a manager. An exception is the relatively recent program in Management of Technology initiated at the Massachusetts Institute of Technology as a co-venture between its engineering and business schools. Rarer yet are programs focused on giving engineers and business people substantive insights into one anothers' professional domains. In the consortia we studied, resources and talent are generally focused on the act of creating technology—rather than on managing its introduction or use. In this sense only one half of the technology agenda is being addressed. The other half goes unattended.

Another Look at the Management of Technology

The issue frames itself this way: American enterprises must rethink the business of managing technology so that, when opportunities arise out of industry-university partnerships, they can tap the potential. "All these changes mean that the corporate structure will need executives who are educated somewhat differently than they are today," says President Richard Cyert of CMU.* Can industry-university consortia help them in this relearning process?

Relearning means redesigning organizations to see over a longer time horizon. It also means distinguishing between technologies that bring new products to the markets and others that improve production processes. And it means accelerating the flow of knowledge and information within organizations that are generally lineal descendants of highly compartmentalized hierarchies.

Look at the Fifth Generation example. In the late 1970s, professors from MIT like Joel Moses, Michael Dertouzos, and Edward Feigenbaum went to U.S. computer manufacturers with the concepts and ideas for the design of a radically new "knowledge processor." These companies failed to see the potential and declined to take on the project. But the ideas were not lost on the Japanese. They quickly saw the merits of the new machine, and in 1979 they startled the world (and the American originators) with the announcement of the Fifth Generation computer project in Tokyo. By the mid-1980s, while many observers had become doubtful about the possibility of the Japanese achieving their goals, few denied that the technological pay-offs, planned or unplanned, would be immense.

How can American industry learn to recognize and tap opportunities faster? Are consortia a mechanism for such learning? So far, the results, while mixed, are not impressive. To date, the measurable impact seems

*"The Plight of Manufacturing," *Issues in Science & Technology* (Summer 1985): p. 98.

minimal although it is too soon to tell. While successful industry-university consortia depend on the support of enlightened high-level managers, many in middle-management ranks remain skeptical about the value of a university connection. At Worcester Polytechnic Institute's robotics program (Manufacturing Engineering Applications Center—MEAC), for example, many middle-level participants from GM and DEC felt that they could have accomplished their immediate objectives more quickly and in the long run more cheaply by going to a "systems house" rather than a university for answers to their problems. Yet the higher level officers weighed positively the benefits in terms of access to personnel and support of the educational system. But are industry-university consortia likely to change the awareness of middle management?

One insight comes from the inner workings of Digital Equipment Corporation (DEC), the nation's second-largest computer manufacturer, headquartered in Maynard, Massachusetts. Higher level corporate attention to consortia began in 1980. The change in DEC's attitude came from international competitive pressures and the end of the IBM antitrust suit. DEC has programs at many universities. The main ones include MIT-Athena; CMU's Artificial Intelligence program and Robotics Institute; Stanford's CIS and Sun-DEC project; Berkeley's CAD/CAM and UNIX projects; Harvard's Pericles Project, which is working on legal expert systems; and others at Columbia, Rensselaer, and Cornell. Magnetics is especially important to DEC, and it participates in magnetics programs at CMU, San Diego, and the University of Wisconsin. The company's external research programs, not only in the United States but abroad, is hardly small. Depending how you value the equipment and services, DEC annually contributes between $50 and more than $100 million annually to them.

With all these investments, how does a company move ideas from academe down through its management ranks? By looking at how technology transfers flow—or better, trickle down—through the inner workings of DEC, the unpredictableness of the process became clear. We learned this from the experiences of a DEC employee in charge of day-to-day relations with MEAC.

The story is told by a thirty-five-year-old DEC engineer, Paul, who is responsible for operational liaison between DEC and MEAC. His description, coming from the insides of DEC, gives one a realistic account of how industry-university partnerships affect industry and how difficult it is to change managerial culture, even in a company like Digital Equipment, which is well known for the quality of its products and for its positive attitudes toward the university community.

"Selling an industry-university partnership is tough. It's frustrating," says Paul. "In a manufacturing environment like this, the guys want to get the product out the door. If it won't help them this week, they don't want to stop for some academic exercise.

"It wasn't logical, like 'we had this problem, let's find somebody to solve it.' We got into MEAC because a VP liked it. He said something to the effect that 'It was a good thing to do.' " But shortly thereafter, the vice president left DEC. His former deputy, Ron Cadieux, filled in for him. DEC joined MEAC in February 1984 and paid the $50,000 subscription fee. Paul was then supposed to get one or more projects launched within DEC, each with additional funding, to take advantage of their membership. Already, five different groups in DEC shared the MEAC fee.

Getting an actual project started wasn't easy. The first proposal fell through. The corporate research group wanted to experiment with an automatic screwdriver driven by an XYZ table, but the group was disbanded before the project was approved. A second false start was a project proposed in DEC's Acton, Massachusetts, offices for the company's Caribbean operation in Puerto Rico. It was put "on hold" because of a reorganization. "The main reason the third project was approved was because the head of our AMT-East group liked the work of one of our WPI summer employees, Bill Krantz," says Paul. "The project was approved because they hoped to hire him."

The AMT-East group joined with the CAEM (Computer Aided Engineering and Manufacturing) group to fund Krantz's research at MEAC. This was the Intelligent Materials Handling Controller—IMHC. It is a small piece of a much larger materials handling project, the piece that adds flexibility to materials handling. "If there's a glitch in the production line and you have to reroute materials, that's what Krantz's IHMC program would do," states Paul.

Will anyone ever use IHMC? Will the technology be transferred? Paul's answer is: "Yes, at the Springfield factory we have a 'plant partner.' It's Irv Winter. He'll use the results of MEAC's work. But he may never know it. He's committed to the FMC (flexible materials handling) project from the CAEM group. He couldn't care less where the flexibility part came from. I don't know if he's ever heard, or cares about, MEAC.''

What is the upshot of the DEC story? First, somehow, the system does work. Technology gets transferred. But it may be working right for the wrong reasons. Second, the system is fragile. A corporate reorganization can quickly unravel the fabric and kill projects. For a university dependent on support this can be traumatic.

But a more pervasive resistance was revealed from further discussions. Although the project started with top management support (the original top manager did leave before the project began), middle managers questioned it. Several of them recommended a systems house or consultant to do the job because their track record and reliability were perceived as higher than MEAC's. Plant level managers and workers neither cared or knew where the innovation came from. The prevailing attitude was ''If it works, use it; otherwise, forget it.'' There were no rewards or incentives for them to think otherwise. The serendipity of personalities and timing had a lot more to do with technology transfer in this case than did enlightened and sustained managerial vision.

Another story, this one from Rensselaer Polytechnic Institute (RPI), illustrates how a consortium arrangement can affect the way industry operates. It is told by Bob Messler, associate director of the Center for Manufacturing Productivity and Technology Transfer in RPI's Jonsson Engineering Center.

''The GE skunk works is in Building H. It's part of the Center for Interactive Computer Graphics. It's making a dent on the structure of industry. GE moved twelve of its engineers out of the Schenectady bureaucracy and housed them at RPI,'' recounts Messler. ''There it joined them with ten to fifteen students and faculty. The goal was to break out of old industry patterns. It's called the 'art to part' program, another name for computer integrated manufacturing. It runs for three years, has $750,000 in cash from GE, which does not include the salaries of the twelve GE engineers.''

The ''cultural'' implications are intriguing. Employees are being shifted out of one culture and into another. They, in turn, will affect (or be affected by) the university world they move into. The payoff may be in new interactions that result between corporate engineers, faculty, students, and other corporate representatives. Forecasting the outcome in measurable terms would, of course, be futile. The process is not quantifiable. One can well imagine, however, the potential for new ideas and new linkages.

If relearning of technology management is a central issue for corporate America, are industry-university consortia changing the rules? Surprisingly the answer is not what one might expect. "They don't change management ways," say both Terry Loucks of the Norton Company and John Wilson of Cincinnati Milacron. Their emphatic answer confirms the fact that consortia, at least those we studied, were not founded with that purpose in mind. On the other hand this may be exactly where there is a gaping hole—or missing piece—to the agenda of R&D consortia.

Chapter 5

RESHAPING ACADEME

There are those believe that universities are institutions frozen in time—or the "ivory-tower" image. Others, would argue that universities are pacesetters of change. Either way, change needs to come fast to the university. The class of 2001 is already in primary school. Remember the year 1970? We are further along the way to the year 2,000 than we are close to 1970. What are some of the fundamental changes required, and to what extent do industry-university consortia highlight some of these pressing issues?

Probably the most important issue concerns the mission of the university. What role should higher education play in today's world? Since there will always be more than a single mission, especially given the nearly 4,000 institutions of higher education in the United States, a better way to phrase the issue is whether more universities should expand their sense of mission to include a direct role in fueling the economy. We speak in terms of the nation's 100 leading research universities at present. Shouldn't we have leading research *and technology* universities? And shouldn't there be more than 100?

In our study of consortia, we found much sympathy for this perspective that a reshaping in academe is badly needed and that one of the primary missions of the university should be a more activist role in the economy. Philosophically, we can trace these roots back to the notion of mixing work and study—all students before they graduate should have opportunities for "real world" experiences. Most do already. We've already mentioned deliberate efforts to do so by Carnegie-Mellon University (CMU) under President Richard Cyert, or at the University of Massachusetts under Chancellor Joseph Duffey. MIT has been and remains committed to that goal. Others exemplify the change underway.

Rensselaer Polytechnic Institute is consciously moving from a *teaching* to a *technology* university. As a teaching university, it dealt primarily with undergraduates. As a technology university, it will be graduate level, research based, and linked to industry. The goals, objectives, procedures, and processes by which this is to take place are carefully mapped out in a visionary document called RPI 2000, the product of the late president, George Low, a charismatic figure who was formerly the head of the Apollo moon mission. RPI's goal is to be one of the premier technology universities in the country, rivaling CalTech, MIT, and CMU. "We realized that if we remained an undergraduate teaching institution, we would not survive as a private school. George Low, the president, showed us that. The RPI Plan 2000 gave us the mission to change," says Chris LeMaistre, director of RPI's Center for Industrial Innovation.

"MIT developed the '6A plan' in 1919," says Professor Linvill. "Undergrads, through master's degrees, coupled practice with education in technology, institutional settings, and engineering. This decreased in intensity when federal funding rose."

"Consortia are throwing us into research that is 'relevant' and basic as opposed to basic 'exploratory,' " says President Cyert. "It means that a whole new group of potential faculty, that otherwise would have gone to industry, will stay on campus. Ten years ago they would have moved on. We are coming around to teaching *to do* things rather than *about* things."

His words are reinforced by his provost, Dr. Jordan. "The pragmatists think we are creating the new fundamentals of engineering science by working with industry. For example, the steam engine came from a need. The same is happening in advanced automation. It involves scientists who don't mind doing technology. The experimental and fundamental are moving together. This creates new paradigms, theorems, conjectures. It advances the state of knowledge." And Professor Robert Ayres, also of

CMU, adds, "clustering of innovator complexes is becoming an explicit role of universities."

What does this mean for universities? How would they have to change to meet the new demands of the twenty-first century?

Entry Level Talent

High skill levels are no longer confined to a special breed of engineers working at the leading edge of technology. Truck drivers today in a well-known courier service drive with computerized information systems at the console of their gearshift. Agents in financial service companies must learn to use "expert systems" as a sales tool. Technicians must use artificial intelligence software in monitoring chemical plant processes. The making and use of technology must involve a greater breadth of people as applications expand.

For the moment, most industry-university consortia concentrate on the 100 leading research universities. This needs to be expanded. According to Ed Cranch, former president of Worcester Polytechnic Institute and now the director of the Wang Institute, we run the danger of widening a two-tier system of education.

> One of the things you see over time is something I describe as the evolution of a two-tiered system of education of engineering and science. Essentially those institutions who have access to these resources we talk about—government and industry money—are getting richer. What this is doing is solidifying a dichotomy between two tiers. You see it when you list all the institutions. Fifty percent of degrees are granted by institutions that are not active at the graduate level. The other fifty percent of BS degrees are by institutions with a significant research component. One of the major questions for the future is the lack of access to these resources being made available. This is a fundamental issue, and it relates to the nation's survival.

Who Educates?

The corporate education budget is now as high as the whole budget of U.S. higher education—or about $60 billion a year. This was confirmed in a recent study from the Carnegie Foundation for the Advancement of

Teaching* Some companies such as AT&T, they pointed out, provide more education and training than the largest university in the world. Commenting on the business and university education role, Frank Newman says: "Equal numbers of people are enrolled. Some 60 to 80 percent of business' education is done in-house. You've got a lot of this going on most of it without any connection to formal education. A lot is remedial in nature as a result of the failure'of educational institutions. On the other hand, on the research front, you get the feeling that somehow we've got to get together. I'm just a little confused about the motives. The roles are getting blurred. What is the future?"

Others agree with the fact that boundary lines are getting fuzzy. As Stanford's Professor Linvill suggests: "Universities and industry are by the nature of the environment we're in—the graduate part of university that is—moving toward the same problems. Industry looks much more like the university. They recognize they've got a majority of their employees who don't know about microprocessors and who must be effective to continue. As a result, they're in education to a degree they've never been before. And in engineering, the university is responding very much to this applied phenomenon. That means engineering. So, we in the university are becoming more like industry whether we really like it or not. Most of us like it. That's why it's becoming very natural for these things to evolve."

Life-Long Learning

Another fundamental change that needs to come to the university is a far greater commitment to lifelong learning. Since the half-life of engineering knowledge is estimated to be five years—meaning that one-half of what engineers learn is obsolete by the time they graduate— then it becomes essential to provide a system whereby the work force can return to academia to renew itself.

Many authorities have zeroed in on the issue of the vast reskilling job ahead in the United States and other countries. "There's a huge installed base of people who need reskilling," says Terry Loucks. "They're a problem when we talk about something as advanced as ·new automation

*Nell Eurich, *Corporate Classroom: The Learning Business*, (Princeton, N.J.: Carnegie Foundation for the Advancement of Teaching, 1983).

48

techniques. Many times we have a management meeting in which we see the proposal and the impact and the cost advantage. Then we have another meeting where we say, 'How can a company known for lifetime employment do this if it puts 30 percent of our people on the streets in a town where they all live?' These people don't go away. It's a community issue. You need management at the top to start saying, 'Alright let's get on with this task of reskilling.' Let's make major dollar investments not only in the hardware and the software but in the knowledgeware. That's probably not going to come out of the engineering school. In these consortia one group is missing: While the one group is automating, the other (missing) group should be changing the human resource base to cope with the new tasks.''

Courses to combat obsolescence have been around for many years. What industry-university consortia raise is the issue of whether or not universities shouldn't be organized for a far greater flow in-and-out between industry and campus. Terry Loucks thinks of the ideal as someone with a ''hopscotch'' resume, someone who has switched back and forth from industry to university and back again.

What's good in relation to the consortia is watching people go back and forth between these worlds. We talk about entrepreneurs being hybrid players. But there are a lot of people who spend a few years in academia and go into industry and go back. And sometimes they take no more with them than knowledge of what the most important problem is. In computer integrated manufacturing, that's happening alot. With two managements groups—industry and academe—there are some benefits there. Cross-education takes place. At MEAC, we encountered installation problems, and we started asking mechanical engineering people why they weren't including computer-science people. Why were they acting independently? That probably had a flow the other direction. Those are hard problems for presidents and deans to solve alone. Sometimes an industry partner asking for a multidisciplinary solution can help to break things down. At RPI, we found someone helping us solve a chemical problem—this from someone with a hopscotch resume.

Cracks in the Departmental Structure?

Another major—very major—issue concerns the structure of the university itself. Nearly every major university is structured into departments—independent political and intellectual domains, some would attest. All tenure, promotion, and reward systems are tied to the department. Any young person, any person, for that matter, seeking a career path in a university has to think first of the department. Department chairman or head is one of the most powerful and influential positions in the university.

There are many good reasons for the preservation of departments. There is the integrity of the methodology and subject matter. There is the need for experts in a particular discipline. But should things remain that way? Is a tightly compartmentalized university or college appropriate to the education of a worldly individual?

Unfortunately, real world problems don't hold still for departmental boundaries. They require interdisciplinary research. Some would call it integrated research. Industry-university consortia are well poised to do such cross-boundary research. The issue is whether they can do so, without the university restructuring itself so that those who work on such projects are not sidetracked out of the departmental promotion and reward system.

At some institutions, Boston University being an example, the only way around the problem is to create autonomous centers that draw faculty from various departments. The problem gets sticky when it comes to issuing degrees—whose department has jurisdiction, and how will accreditation be affected?

But the desire and pressure for integration is there, and it is strong. Dr. George Pake, a vice president of research at Xerox, spoke of Stanford's Center for Integrated Systems (CIS). "We wanted to create an 'integrated center.' This would bring related disciplines under one roof. Especially computer science and engineering. These weren't as deeply involved as they should be. There's a hope that other parts of the university will come together at CIS. Systems architecture is the weakest part. There's a cultural gap between hardware and software people. It's hard to overcome that. This was my principal aim. Chip makers see this problem. Academics don't."

The emphasis on interdisciplinary work is linked to 'real problems,' "
argues President Richart Cyert. "The world doesn't give you problems
neatly packaged." The view is supported by James Williams, head of
engineering at CMU: "Over the next twenty years more important and
more exciting problems will be interdisciplinary—in contrast to pure
science and narrow focus such as at Yale or Princeton."

Another facet of the argument favoring the dismantling departmental
barriers is the debate over the "ideal" characteristics of an entry-level
worker moving from academe to industry. Employers often—and fairly—
argue that employees coming directly from universities are poorly
prepared for the realities of work life. In many cases, a superior student
in engineering or science is inadequately prepared in the written or spoken
use of English, in organizational behavior, or in management. Others
have little idea of what is required of them in a working environment. Part
of the reason is that few students are encouraged to engage in studies
beyond departmental walls or beyond the bounds of the university. One
effect—and a costly one—is to shift an educational burden onto employers.

"The perfect situation," says Larry Hollingshead of Cincinnati
Milacron, "is to have a student walk into work and not miss a beat." This
is what ensued as a result of Cincinnati Milacron's participation in
CIDMAC's interdisciplinary joint venture with industry. "We've hired
our first three students from the project and they were up to speed within
days at Cincinnati Milacron. They had already been into our manufacturing plants because they were studying 'real-life problems.' In prior
cases it might have been a matter of months or weeks."

Other pressures for change are unavoidable. Look at MIT's Project
Athena, directed by Steve Lerman. "One of the overriding goals is
'coherence'—increasing the possibility of sharing information across the
entire campus. What we are trying to do is to revolutionize the way
learning is delivered at MIT." Many different departments are involved
in Project Athena. Will it change the departmental structure? Unlikely,
according to the project's administrators. At MIT, at least, that would be
too ambitious. But it does get people from one department talking to
people from another.

This interdisciplinarity has both its problems and its limits. One
problem was expressed by Mary Johnson, the manager of corporate

relations for RPI's Center for Interactive Computer Graphics: "The problem is that the academic structure does not reward properly. Young faculty are nervous working in the center because it doesn't count toward tenure. Older, established faculty don't need the money, they can raise research funds on their own. This is the single greatest issue that we're trying to break down," she observes.

"On the issue of rewards, RPI is fighting the faculty-researcher split," observes Johnson. "Student researchers carry the title 'graduate research assistant.' Then we have professional researchers called 'research assistants' and 'research associates.' The meagre distinction between a graduate student and a professional is pretty thin if you look at the titles. And the nuance is not lost on professional researchers.

"The problem," she adds, "is there is no academic career path for them, they have no stature under the old university reward system and are ineligible for tenure which is given by a home department. Either they go to industry (and we lose them) or they get frustrated with second class status. We have to find a way to solve this. There needs to be a dual career ladder, one for professors and one for researchers."

If change comes to the university—at least the kind we have discussed here—it will deeply impact its sense of mission and its inner workings. But, as we have already stated the same process of change must envelop the business enterprise if it too completes its own transition from one economic era to another. The issues they faced are crystallized in part by our reflections on consortia and questions of controlling research and understanding the business of technology transfer. Together, these perspectives help us better focus on the issue as a matter of national concern.

It is clear that we are being challenged—partly from outside by competitors, partly from within by our inability to adapt fast enough. It is equally clear, however, that one of our unique strengths is our vast and varied system of higher education. Since industry-university consortia are the most direct meeting point between higher education and the economy, is there any evidence that they are beginning to exert pressure, even if ever so slight, on the structure of the university? And correspondingly, are there signs that executives are beginning to respond to the new challenges of learning to manage technology better?

The industry-university consortia phenomenon is still too new, at least in its present form, to venture definitive answers to such all-encompassing questions. Nonetheless, our research yields several observations. (1) A new research agenda is being formed, jointly by university and industry. (2) A new climate for the transfer of technology is being created, in as many ways as there are consortia. The shortcoming here may have more to do with "management of technology" in the enterprise than with the creation of technology in our laboratories. (3) The university is responding, slowly and often two steps forward, one step back. But what seemed like a novelty in 1980—companies on campus—is rapidly becoming the norm. There will be "more Stanfords than Yales." Will the Stanfords start restructuring themselves? Some will, some will not. The strength of our system is that there is room for both. But industry-university consortia certainly lead to water, whether it will be drunk or not.

The discussion in the previous three chapters has led us through the broader implications of the consortia phenomenon. But there is another task to which we now turn. Do industry-university consortia work? What are the mechanics involved in creating successful consortia?

Part III
THE
MECHANICS

Chapter 6

WHY CREATE A CONSORTIUM?

Modern architectural theory suggests that the ideal building is one in which form follows function. The same might be said of consortia. The final form or structure they are given should—ideally—follow the function expected of them. Thus, when Governor James Hunt of North Carolina rationalized the creation of a microelectronics consortium to his legislature, he did it by arguing that its function would be to leverage economic growth in the Research Triangle Park. It was logical, therefore, to see the Department of Commerce as the parent institution through which funding was channeled to the Microelectronics Center of North Carolina (MCNC). And it was logical to see the MCNC designed in such a way that it would be a magnet for industries to locate near it by sharing its resources, and that it be a catalyst for strengthening the quality of education in area universities by sharing equipment, laboratories, staff, and a communications network.

In contrast, the Center for Integrated Systems (CIS) at Stanford was less concerned about explaining itself as a job generator to state politicians. Rather it focused on creating a new alliance between two disciplines that rarely worked together as day-to-day collaborators: electrical engineering and computer science. Business executives and university faculty set out to design a program, a building, and an environment that would achieve the function of integrating academic disciplines. They worried little about direct job creation and lot more about the intellectual atmosphere of the Center.

These two examples underscore an important point about the founding and molding of a consortium. The functional motives, if well explained and well understood, will lead to the form. This explains why no two consortia are alike, a frustration for those looking for a replicable model. At Purdue University, Professor James Solberg found out the futility of looking for a model in the early stages of helping to create the Computer Integrated Design, Manufacturing, and Automation Center (CIDMAC). "When we were forming our center, we were looking for some secret formula of success. We never found anything like that. I'm convinced there's no single formula for success," he concluded.

What are some of the primary functional motives? Our study of fourteen consortia, and of others in lesser depth, suggests five main categories. In practice there can be more than one motive involved, itself an explanation of the complexity many of the consortia arrangements can take. The five include (1) strengthening universities, (2) stimulating economic growth, (3) engaging in basic research, (4) creating generic technologies, or (5) developing and delivering specific products.

Strengthening Universities

Strengthening universities by supporting engineering or science programs is a driving motive of many of the new R&D consortia. By supplying capital construction monies, operating funds, equipment, or shared experts, consortia partners hope to affect the character and quality of technical education services. Examples include initiating new interdisciplinary research programs such as those at Carnegie-Mellon's Robotics Institute or integrating academic fields as at Stanford's CIS. For sponsoring companies, the product of such efforts is both a higher caliber graduate who might be employed by consortia sponsors and leading-edge research and development.

The Microelectronics Center in Massachusetts, funded by the state and private matching donations, defines itself as a supporting resource for universities by providing equipment. Although the Center makes no presumptions about interfering in academics' research priorities, it does expect to channel more engineers into process engineering of semiconductors. Project Athena at MIT and the IBM project at Carnegie-Mellon are cases of technology transfer to universities of large equipment donations and technological know-how. Here too, a principal motive for industry is the development of better educated specialists; new technology creation is next. For the university, one objective is to affect its own educational technologies. In both cases, this means networking campuses with high-powered computer work stations.

The broader context behind efforts to strengthen universities—and one we described at length in *Global Stakes*—is the weakened state of engineering education in the United States. Capacity is still an issue. Enrollments remain capped. Equipment is outdated. Faculty are in demand with vacancies running high. Classes are overcrowded. Buildings are old. And the best graduate students are quickly lured away to higher paying industry jobs, a process that undermines the research strength of a university. The result of this drain is a graduate enrollment with foreign nationals constituting more than one-half the total. Such circumstances require more than ad hoc fix-it efforts. In this regard, the consortium effort offers the positive option of sustained funding in amounts large enough to make a qualitative difference. With further cutbacks in sight from federal sources as a national deficit-cutting cycle goes into effect, even more pressure may fall on consortia-type arrangements to fill the university funding vacuum.

One problem signaled by efforts cast around the motive of strengthening universities is that their principal achievements may be to do exactly that—and nothing else. If, as argued in earlier chapters, the university itself must change to be a more effective participant in furthering economic growth then change must go beyond just being "stronger" or doing "more of the same." If, on the other hand, consortia efforts focused on aiding university lead to improved mechanisms for technology transfer, reduced departmental barriers, or greater interchange between industry and academe then the longer term effects might prove more economically and intellectually substantial.

Stimulating Economic Growth

Promoting regional economic growth is common motive for creating R&D consortia. This goal is most frequently rationalized by government-initiated collaborative arrangements. Examples include the Microelectronics Center of North Carolina, the Industrial Technology Institute in Michigan, the Corporation for Science and Technology in Indiana, and the Centers of Advanced Technology in New York and New Jersey. Their public sector promoters frequently cast their expectations from these consortia in terms of employment. Jobs, after all, are nirvana to politicians on the campaign trail.

In Pennsylvania, the creation of the Benjamin Franklin program was passed through the legislature with the uncontested belief that jobs would quickly materialize rapidly from funds targeted for technology projects. Since March 1983, $50 million in state monies have stimulated matching commitments of $169 million from private sources. State officials point to 4,600 jobs created or retained as one measure of their achievement. The same argument helped carry the MCNC through the North Carolina political process and later the Corporation for Science and Technology through the Indiana legislature.

We are "paving the way to future Indiana jobs," states a CST brochure. Seven projects approved for funding in October 1985 will lead to 450 new jobs in three to five years. "CST awardees now report planned expenditures in excess of $410 million," says Dr. John Hague, CST president, "in support of projects made possible by the first $20 million CST invested during the first biennium." For Indiana, this is heady news.

To target on jobs alone, however, is misleading. R&D is not a linear process that terminates in a short time with predictable numbers of new jobs. R&D is an ongoing, long-term process with jobs coming only as a by-product of a successfully executed R&D initiative. Putting jobs first can stymie the R&D effort if expectations are focused solely on the short-term, year-to-year employment payoff.

This was a trap Governor Michael Dukakis of Massachusetts fell into when he saw an opportunity "to create jobs" by locating the state's new microelectronics center in an economically depressed town. Industrial supporters of the center argued against the site on the simple grounds that no useful R&D would happen there because it was too far from the locus of industrial activity. "No one would show up," they said. Fortunately the governor lost that round.

On the other hand, doing it right, while it is risky, offers enormous return. Aware that North Carolina would fund the MCNC was a deciding factor in GE's spending $100 million at Research Triangle Park and setting up shop in the semiconductor business there. Other firms were soon attracted to locate nearby.

Many people naturally raise doubts about the policies of competing states, all trying to raise their employment levels by focusing too narrowly on what they label as high-tech industry. Marc Tucker, for example, notes "All too many states are more or less agreed that their economic future is assured if they have a high-tech center, a research park (a.k.a speculative real estate development), and a policy to provide free vocational training. That's the package being developed. If the centers are viewed only as 'high tech' there is a strict limit to how many can be supported. If in one state after another governors and legislators ask themselves how they can help their existing industrial base by making efficient use of leading edge technology, that would be a whole other matter. But that doesn't seem to be what they are doing. That's what worries me." The reality is, however, that this approach is taking root in states like Michigan or Ohio where it is well understood that new technologies are the key to rejuvenating old industries.

Just how tricky the state-jobs issue can be was illustrated by a case at Rensselaer Polytechnic Institute (RPI). Rensselaer runs an incubator program. The idea is that to attract top faculty to RPI, they need an outlet for their entrepreneurial activities. They can start a company in the incubator space—as can students—and then move to the Rensselaer Technology Park. There are currently fifteen companies in the incubator space housed, appropriately perhaps, in a building once used as a home for wayward girls. Ironically, the most successful incubator company was Raster Technologies, founded by two RPI grad students. Instead of moving out into the RPI Park, it moved to Boston! Why? "Because," explains Jerry Mahone, the director, "when they had to grow overnight from 3 to 60 employees, they found the other 57 qualified people in Boston. Also, all their competition and suppliers were there. In the end," continues Mahone, "it was a blessing in disguise, because now people had to work a hell of a lot harder not to lose fledgling high-tech industries to another region."

Engaging in Basic Research

A third motive for creating R&D consortia is to pool resources in funding costly long-term pure research in fields that are of potential commercial importance. The Semiconductor Research Corporation (SRC) exemplifies this approach. Its goal was to take the lead in determining the national agenda in semiconductor research. The SRC acts as a funding conduit for pooled corporate monies that are used to contract university-based research. Behind this motive is a recognition of a changing federal agenda moving away from commercially attractive research.

The problem with industry stepping in to mount a national program commensurate in scale to federal R&D programs is that the financial demands would far exceed its means. At present, no more than 5 percent of university-based R&D is industrially supported. This represents a 40 percent jump over three years, but it still falls far short of the need. About 66 percent of university R&D is federal. A drop of 5 to 10 percentage points would be calamitous.

Another problem for industry, even if it combines resources in collaborative programs, is one of endurance. Business cycles. Acquisitions. Changing senior executive positions. Such changes can cause havoc to R&D investments made outside of a corporation. They are often the "first to go" when cost-cutters take hold or strategies are reshuffled. In contrast, during the post-war period one can see the immense impact of federal initiative that endured for ten-to twenty-year periods. Funding of computer science research out of the Advanced Research Projects Agency (ARPA) of the Department of Defense is a case in point. But that effort is rapidly getting politicized by the growing momentum of the Strategic Defense Initiative (SDI). In its wake other programs are withering.

It would appear, therefore, that consortia aside from exceptions such as the massive Bellcore grouping or the SRC may be unable to marshall the resources required to sustain the university-based basic research establishment in the United States. This means that creation of research consortia building, as evidenced in the National Science Foundation's recent experiment with Engineering Research Centers, may have to become an explicit federal priority with a goal of inviting in industry, state, or foundation partners. The nation's network of federal laboratories might be able to make such a transition with adequate vision and proper industry participation.

Creating Generic Technologies

A fourth motive involved in creating an R&D consortium is to develop generic technologies useful to a broad cross-section of industrial sponsors. An example of a technology might be the evolution of computer-aided design concepts or computer-integrated manufacturing, which are then developed into products or processes by the sponsoring firm. Another might be analyses of new materials behavior such as polymers or ceramics with product creation left, again, to individual corporations. The motive for pooling resources is the need to invest in large development costs, oftentimes stretching over a period of years.

CIDMAC at Purdue, the Microelectronics and Computer Technology Corporation (MCC), the Rensselaer complex of consortia, the Robotics Institute at Carnegie-Mellon, and the Ceramics Center at Rutgers fall into this category. So does the SRC. Its goal, says Larry Sumney, executive director, is "the establishment of a major, focused, generic research program that will be supportive of the long-term research needs of the semiconductor industry; secondly, providing more relevant graduate education and a larger supply of graduate students; and thirdly, helping to improve communication within the entire semiconductor industry."

Developing Specific Products

Finally, another motive for creating a consortia is to develop specific products or services. In such cases, the consortium works under contract to its corporate client and commits to deliver a well-defined product. The combined resources of consortia members supports the overhead and generic research while specific contracts might call for the creation of deliverable products.

The Robotics Institute at Carnegie-Mellon is an example. Although it engages in abstract generic research and development, it works with individual partners to deliver working tools or technologies. In one case, the Robotics Institute was contracted to produce, under tight deadlines, several operational robots for use within contaminated areas of the Three Mile Island nuclear power plant. The Manufacturing Engineering Applications Center (MEAC) at Worcester Polytechnic Institute is another case of client companies wanting the product "loaded on a truck" and delivered. At MEAC, a "dumb" robot arrives on a laboratory floor where it is then programmed to perform "intelligent" customized tasks. It is then sent out again to work on a shop floor.

But asking a faculty person and an entourage of graduate students to learn as they go on projects that are needed for delivery under tight, cost-effective deadlines is not always possible. As a result, this approach to consortia building is often criticized for trying to do something for which commercial consultants might be far better equipped to do. A broader view might argue that there is a "learning curve" benefit of having new generations be exposed to solving "real-life" problems. This argument is not always persuasive—as we noted in an earlier description of technology transfer at DEC—with middle managers who are under pressure to function within tightly prescribed boundaries.

Expectations

What can we—or should we—expect of R&D consortia? The motives we've explored provide some answers. For the present, to expect them to become *the* principal medium for subsidizing or setting the nation's pure research agenda seems fanciful. Similarly, to expect that these same consortia can be the primary catalyst for stimulating the creation of coveted high-tech jobs or just simply jobs may themselves be unrealistic expectations.

A more appropriate framework for judging their value may come from stepping back to Part II and reconsidering the questions of control over research, technology transfer, and structural change in academe as "ends" in and of themselves. Seen in this light, consortia take on a different meaning as catalysts of change. How successful they are in doing so is influenced by their operational mechanics or, in different words, by their idiosyncracies. These involve choices that mirror the familiar dictum that form should follow function. That's why a grant-making consortium, like the Corporation for Science and Technology, concerned with job creation, looks and acts far differently than a profit-making consortium that carries out its own research, like the MCC, or one such as the SRC that sets a precise research agenda and contracts out tasks to universities.

Our study of R&D consortia suggested four categories of choices that, once made, determine the consortia's operational form: (1) Partners—Who will they be? (2) Money and Influence—How much and with what strings? (3) The Agenda—What are the research goals and who determines them? And (4) Leadership—Who leads and what image is projected?

Within each of the four categories are subsets of choices. We present these by juxtaposing opposites. For example, "Do I include many partners or few partners?" In reality, the final decision may fall somewhere between two plausible extremes. Thus, the choice between including "big company partners versus small company partners" might in fact end up with a partnership of large and small companies such as is the case with the Carnegie-Mellon Robotics Institute. Or, trying to decide whether to address "a regional agenda versus a national agenda" one may in fact start, as was the case in North Carolina's Microelectronics Center, with the former as far as jobs and economic growth goes and quickly evolve to the latter in terms of research. The four subsequent chapters take each of these four categories as a heading.

Chapter 7

PARTNERS

Who should belong to a consortium? The answers depends in large part on who takes the initiative and what the motives are behind doing so. A few years ago, Erich Bloch, then a vice president for Technical Personnel Development at IBM, determined that U.S. semiconductor makers and users were not meeting the Japanese challenge and that federal research dollars were not being channeled to respond to this threat. "I am tempted to cite the diplomat who cabled from one of his missions," he wrote in a Semiconductor Industry Association publication in 1983, " 'It's impossible to exaggerate the seriousness of the situation—but I'll try.' "

Bloch's reaction was to lobby among his corporate peers for the creation of a research consortium. This took him to the most obvious prospects: large makers and users of semiconductors who had big R&D budgets from which to allocate the sums needed. The choice, in other consortia cases, is not always that obvious nor the linkage between partners that compelling.

Many Partners vs Few Partners

One of the first issues is whether there should be many or few partners. RPI has over fifty corporate members, the largest number of any of the consortia we studied. The RPI program is impressive. As summarized earlier, it consists of three interlinked programs: interactive computer graphics, manufacturing productivity, and integrated electronics. One of the programs has thirty-eight members alone. In contrast, Project Athena at MIT has only two large corporate members—IBM and DEC (although Codex and Bolt, Beranek, and Newman also have some involvement). What are the advantages or disadvantages of many versus few?

The most compelling reason for including a larger number of partners is to lower the risk—the risk that by dropping out some might jeopardize the whole venture. This indeed has been the case at RPI, where corporate membership has changed from time to time, but the overall budgetary levels have continued to grow. In other cases such as the Robotics Center at the University of Rhode Island, however, large numbers of partners have come and gone, and the budgets have had wide swings in size, despite the many partners. In this case, however, the issue was one of leadership. The two major leaders of the Rhode Island partnership departed for jobs in industry, and with them left much of the direction of the consortium. With a leadership vacuum, many companies chose not to stay, and their large numbers did nothing to prevent budgets from going from a high of $2.7 million down to less than $0.5 million. Now under new leadership of Herman Viets, the program is on the upswing again.

On the other hand, it might seem that fewer partners would extract added energy from the combined group—or else the slowdown of one holds up the works for the rest. This seems particularly true at the MCNC, where the complementary nature of each corporate participant intensifies the interdependence. At MIT's Athena project, both IBM and DEC have several employees on campus at all times, with offices directly located on Athena premises. Their presence attests to their commitment, even though some questions are raised about the slowness of their delivery of 500 as yet undelivered and long-promised IBM work stations. In the interim, the cumulative effect of other equipment donations alone is dramatic. By the end of 1985, 5,000 students became eligible for computer access accounts allowing time on 43 VAXs with 300 terminals and 30 VAX stations and yet another 300 PC ATs and XTs.

At Carnegie-Mellon, the slowness of commitment on the part of the single partner IBM obliged the academic vice president to try and expand the number of partners—a multivendor strategy—to induce more commitment. Pat Crecine said of this dilemma: "We have a dramatic relationship with IBM. We're a beta test site for a wide range of manufacturers. Every major research university is doing this. There's an uneasy relationship. DEC, IBM, Apple, Sun. Dealing with these different organizations... we're trying to influence them and they are trying to sell you what they want to anyway. It's fascinating."

The case at the Optics Institute of the University of Rochester is interesting. There were four founding company members: Kodak, Xerox, Bausch & Lomb, and Corning. Two more, IBM and GE, joined later. What's interesting is that the first four joined on a handshake with the president but three of them made little effort to participate in the program. The one exception was Kodak which has three campus-based employees actively involved in the program. So here is a case where there are few members, and relatively little active involvement in the research.

At RPI, where there are many companies involved, each pays a correspondingly smaller sum of money for membership—$50,000 per year for a program at the Center for Manufacturing Productivity and Technology Transfer. But at MCC, where there are also a large number of companies—twenty-one and still growing—each new member has to commit more funds, now up to $1 million, purely for membership. Then there are program fees for each of four programs, all of which may translate into a multimillion-dollar investment for each participant.

Many or few? The results are mixed. No clear pattern emerges. Having many partners can ensure against the risk of a budgetary roller coaster but sometimes it does not. Fewer partners increases the active involvement of members but sometimes not. The lesson may be that if there is a pattern, it is that with few partners the commitment level is high, the proprietary nature of the work strong, and the sharing of information in the project restricted. For universities, particularly those with sensitivities about restrained academic freedom, when there are multiple partners projects are likely to be more open and the results less proprietary.

Large Companies vs Small Companies

A persistent and nagging question is how to get the small company involved in a consortium. Since many R&D collaboratives are established to pool a critical mass of funds, an implicit assumption is that only those with sufficient money to make a difference, meaning big companies, need apply. Of the MCC, John Lacey, its Vice President for Technology and Planning, says that it is open to "those engaged in substantial research and development in microelectronics and computer-related fields in the United States." Indeed, if the entry fee is measured in hundreds of thousands or in some cases in millions of dollars, membership is quickly narrowed to an exclusive club. Thus, there arises a dilemma involving fears of antitrust scrutiny because of the implied exclusionary practices.

"Our job," says Don Beilman, president of the MCNC, "is not profit but technology access with state funding. We need a program at the national level to open new technology to small businesses." Yet even at the MCNC, direct recipient of almost $40 million state dollars (and another $40 million to partner universities), where the corporate entry fee is $250,000 for each of three years, the small business participant has yet to be seen. "Access of small companies is a concern of ours," admits Beilman.

Most of the consortia we studied listed Fortune 500 names as corporate partners. Several centers, however, actively sought ways to involve small companies. Two in New York State are good examples. One is the Optics Institute at the University of Rochester. "One of my major activities in the Center and of my Laser Lab," explains Steve Jacobs, leader of the Optical Materials Group "is to help small companies. We publish research results quickly for small companies. That is part of our proposal to New York State."

A second example is RPI's Incubator program. The program started in 1980 in a basement. The Institute floated a $700,000 bond issue with the City of Troy and got another $200,000 loan. Now it has 40,000 square feet of floor space rented out. The list of companies is intriguing: Among the twenty current ones are names such as Mentor Technologies, Automated Dynamics, QC3 Associates, PEACH, PlayNet, Inc., and Mirror Images Software. About one-third come from campus, one-third are existing small companies, and one-third are parts of larger companies that are spin-offs, especially from GE.

How can one achieve a proper balance among large and small participants? One example is the Robotics Institute at Carnegie-Mellon. Its mid-1985 membership of twenty-eight companies includes the largest such as Westinghouse that spends $1 million per year, to the very small such as Oberg Manufacturing Company that hasn't any cash to offer. Westinghouse contracts for specific research or technology products; Oberg hasn't the resources to do so but did get the right to "look in on" what the Institute is doing.

Oberg Industries is situated about thirty miles northeast of Pittsburgh in a small town—"just beyond the range of unions," one executive noted. It employs about 300 people in making high-precision tool and die products. No bigger than a loaf of bread, these sell at costs of $100,000 or more. They are used to stamp out of metal sheets up to 10,000,000 small and precise parts before being retooled. Oberg is known worldwide for the high quality of its products. But it is under increasing foreign pressure.

The firm would like to reduce the 3,000 to 4,000 skilled man-hours required to make a die in order to compete against a 60 to 70 percent Japanese cost advantage. It could use CAD technologies and better computer systems to control or monitor its precision tooling operations. But the cost is too high. "We just don't have a large staff," says Executive Vice President David O. Shondeck. "What can we digest from a CMU? We don't have people we can send. They're all working on daily assignments."

People may be one problem. Money is another. But thanks to Pennsylvania's technology grants initiative, the Benjamin Franklin Program, administered by CMU (one of four universities to do so in the state), a grant of $30,000 was earmarked to Oberg conditional on a matching obligation by the firm. Oberg in turn contributed about 500 to 1000 hours of machine-tool time to the Institute.

This money and machine time started the firm's involvement in June 1982. The subsidy allowed Oberg to sit in on monthly meetings to view technical reports in various robotics fields. But still there was no way to bring the new technologies into the firm. There weren't any bodies actually handling the technology transfer. After complaints and external pressure from influential friends, the Robotics Institute finally designated two students to work on CAD-related technology at Oberg. To Shondeck this is better than nothing: "It's the only game in town. Either we participate fully or not at all." Some serendipity ("That might have happened anyway") sweetened the relationship somewhat. Oberg teamed with another firm, American Robot, as a result of an introduction engineered by Raj Reddy, the Institute's director. A new product was developed by the two firms. A lot more should probably be happening if Oberg is to stay ahead of Japanese and Korean competitors. But that's problematic. There isn't enough skilled staff, time, or money.

Hall Industries is a Pittsburgh machine tooling firm one-half Oberg's size. Its antiquated Pittsburgh shop employs only sixty people; other divisions are more advanced technologically. The company matches a $7,500 grant of the Benjamin Franklin program. Harold Hall, the company's president, believes in the importance of his investment. "We're in for some hard cash," he says. "If I can get just a few of my people exposed to the Robotics Institute, something will come out of it." Once a month four of his employees spend a day at the Robotics Institute. "I'm asking them to look into tool-sensor devices and to absorb new technologies of any kind."

Several hundred miles away, the Industrial Technology Institute (ITI) in Ann Arbor, Michigan, wrestles with the same problem. Created by the state in 1980 to function as an R&D resource in automated manufacturing technologies, the original goal was to serve a multitude of small auto-supplying firms too lean, too tradition bound, and too understaffed to do anything about modernization. Within fifty miles of the ITI are 7,000 manufacturing firms, principally small suppliers to Detroit's big three auto manufacturers. All—although the firms themselves didn't know it—are potential clients of the new ITI. The most important challenge for the Institute, it states in its original prospectus several years back, is to help those firms that "do not possess in-house the technology development tradition or the resources to deal effectively with the variety of technical problems confronting them, even if they are aware of those problems."

But, five years after the founding of ITI by Governor Milliken in 1980, the "small business" mission is on hold in favor of contractual relations with giants such as GM and Ford that can provide the large sums needed to mount a serious R&D effort. "We just couldn't go after $50,000 a shot from small manufacturers," comments Jerome Smith, the Institute's president. "I've been suppressing the idea of being a consortium. It permits companies to get off the hook. They give a few dollars and no more. Also, in manufacturing it's harder to come together with any consensus. You couldn't pay the freight for things that are nebulous to them."

Some of these concerns are what led James Koontz and others (including Jerome Smith who sits on Koontz's coordinating committee for the National Center for Manufacturing Sciences) to try and work out a formula that would be attractive to small companies with modest resources. But for the moment, one of the big agenda items at ITI is to develop "digital communications standards" needed for computers to talk effectively to large numbers of machines. The sponsors are governmental agencies and big corporations. For the 7,000 small supplier firms, the painful shakeout from intensified competition goes on unabated.

One solution to the "too small" problem, partly illustrated by the Benjamin Franklin Program in Pennsylvania, is exemplified by the Corporation for Science and Technology (CST) in Indianapolis, Indiana. Established by the state with an annual $10 million budget, one of its principal tasks is to contract R&D funds out to individuals, small enterprises, and industry-university joint ventures. Its long-term goal is jobs for Indiana through accelerated diffusion of technology. Its strategy is three-pronged. It commits monies where they might otherwise not go, e.g., to the small entrepreneur in a garage, in a university lab, or an up-and-coming corporation. A second track offers business counsel and a third acts as a broker of technology resource and information. The CST's first president, Alden McLellan IV, defined the organization's goals as follows: "CST is mission oriented but not technology specific. Transfer of technology is the key. We want to see new ideas created and transferred into the marketplace."

In June 1985, the new president, John D. Hague, proudly announced its "First Project to Finish" out of thirty-five funded during the initial eighteen month life of the CST. In this case, a blind programmer, William L. Grimm, founded his own company to produce aids for the sightless. With CST support, he designed what is described as "an extremely portable, self-contained microcomputer with a high resolution voice." Its voice not only reads what is stored but it can spot mistyped words and incorrect computer commands. His product, called Small Talk, sells for $2,000. Annual sales were first projected to grow to $1,000,000 by 1988. Initial monthly sales exceeded original estimates and on October 1, 1985, a first payback was made to CST—a proud moment for all concerned.

Examples such as these, matched against their opposites, such as the MCC and its large corporate members, are testimony to formulae that can successfully address the issue of small business involvement. The doors need not be closed. Public funding can be instrumental, however, in creating opportunities by bringing the needed "money" to the table. That indeed is the lesson of the CST or the Ben Franklin programs and more recently the Thomas Edison program in Ohio.

Complementary Partners vs Competing Partners

We've had a hard time digesting the people from industry and they wonder what the hell we're up to. We've been having a weekly luncheon and we set it up unstructured at the beginning. It was an amazing thing. The first time we met, some of them wondered if they should be caught in this bed with their competitors.

That's the way Professor John Linvill began a conversation on the subject of competing company partners. One might have assumed, as we did prior to this study, that there would be strong distinguishing characteristics between consortia that had competing and those with noncompeting partners. The former might prove tight-lipped and restrained, the latter open to extensive interaction. The reality proved less obvious.

Atmosphere, climate, environment, and attitude are words that often crop up in discussion about how best to structure an R&D consortium. What's the climate like when partners are in competition with one another? It's not what one might think. Take Project Athena, for example. The partners include DEC, which is in direct competition with IBM. Indeed, there was even competition as to who would get the "honor" of working with MIT. Yet, the atmosphere is cordial and cooperative.

In other situations, like MEAC at Worcester Polytechnic Institute, the partners have been as diverse as GE, General Motors, DEC, Norton (an abrasives company), and Emhart (shoe-making machinery, glass bottle machinery, and other industrial products.) But they shared an interest in robots but seldom interacted with one another. As one DEC person noted, "We're too different. We might do a project on robots for miniature microelectronics assembly. GM use huge robots for arc welding. There's no connection. We'll never arc weld a tiny read/write head."

Two of the largest consortia are the SRC and the MCC. Both are composed largely of competing partners. But the two have completely different atmospheres. The SRC partners can be likened to "birds of a feather" and as peaceful as a bevy of doves. The MCC is more akin to a huge farm with chickens and foxes all carefully shepherded by a forceful, watchful, former CIA deputy director.

Thus, the question of competing or noncompeting partners proves to be subtle. It's not just a question of whether or not they compete but whether there is synergy among the partners. The best example of a successful mix is the MCNC, where the four companies form what we might term a "vertically integrated consortium." MCNC's initial four complementary sponsors included a semiconductor manufacturer (GE), an equipment maker (Northern Telecom), a maker of semiconductor manufacturing equipment (GCA), and a supplier of manufacturing process gases (AIRCO). Each stood to gain from having their equipment or knowledge tested in the the manufacturing lab. Each could be counted on to collaborate with the others since none was in competition with the other. Implicit in the arrangement was the cultivation of a collegial atmosphere without fear of losing control over proprietary information.

Most of the other partnerships are mixed. Some companies compete, some don't. Take the Rochester Optics program for example. Is IBM a competitor to Corning Glass? No, not in the traditional sense. On the other hand, they could be potential competitors in fiber optics. Or look at Rutger's Ceramics Center—does its partner W.R. Grace (chemicals) compete with AT&T Technologies (another partner)? No, not at all. Yet another Rutgers partner is Allied Corp., a direct competitor to Grace, and another one is GTE, which is both a competitor and a supplier to AT&T.

Only four of the consortia seemed to consist entirely of direct competitors—MIT Athena, SRC, MCC, and CIS. The antitrust pressures at SRC and MCC were so strong as to call for special presidential dispensations or federal legislation to alleviate, although not eliminate, the fear of antitrust as it applies to R&D partnerships.

The matter of who joins, how large they are, and whether they compete or not leads in turn to issues of money: How much influence and what kind of involvement is expected from those paying the bills? We turn now to this subject.

Chapter 8

MONEY & INFLUENCE

If someone asked what the most efficient formula for financing a consortium is, the answer would be: There is none. There are some basic issues, however. One has to do with how big an investment is required and from whom. State money, for example, may come with less strings than industry money; and it may come in far larger amounts. Or, if minimal direct involvement is intended from corporate partners, how can it be achieved and still raise large sums of capital? And there is also the difficult decision on whether or not to include the federal government particularly if it comes with ''national security'' constraints. The answers are far from obvious.

Small Investment vs Large Investment

Related to an earlier question of company size, biggest versus the smallest, is the matter of how big a supporting contribution a corporate partner might make. To one company, a $1 million investment may represent only a small fraction of its total R&D budget; to another it may represent a huge proportion. Size is relative. Thus if a partner's contribution is large in relation to its total R&D budget, its investment will take on special importance. The implications for a consortium are significant.

A company making a relatively small investment, such as GE Semiconductors' $250,000 a year commitment to the MCNC, allows it to treat the investment as expendable. By hedging its bets on many small R&D investments probability of reward is increased. If any one project fails, little damage is done. At the other extreme, if a company buys into the MCC at a multimillion dollar level, the pressure for results may be linked to its strategic agenda. For this reason, Don Beilman, of the MCNC in North Carolina, is critical of the MCC in Texas: "At MCC all the companies are in the pot. At MCNC, we bring industry in to complement us cooperatively. If you've got a $5 million investment in MCC, you have a much greater vested interest. This creates a very different working environment. If a company has a big stake in a big project, privacy of research becomes a big issue."

Where the investment is smaller a more relaxed and open environment is likely; the investment is implicitly low risk. The bigger the stake, the greater becomes the involvement by a company in research in progress. In the MCC case, the climate is more highly charged and results-minded. Finding the right balance is part of what gives unique character to a particular consortium. Deciding which is the more fertile results-minded environment is probably impossible.

Third-party—or neutral—money may be the key to creating the balance between a pressure-cooker lab and one that is more insulated from day-to-day competitive tensions. By third party we mean an entity that has no interest in actively influencing the administration or research of the particular consortium. Third-party support can mean government money, such as New Jersey State's support for the Ceramics Center at Rutgers (which also receives federal money via the National Science Foundation), or foundation money such as the contributions to ITI from the Kellogg Foundation and the Dow Foundation. The amounts have to be large enough to allow the corporate partner to enter at a low risk. This is the case at the MCNC, where a state contribution of $80 million to the Center and its allied universities is almost ten times greater than what industry is contributing.

An interesting twist on third-party money is at Stanford University's CIS. In this case, it comes from industry, which one would have expected to want a direct involvement. Twenty companies donated a total of $15,000,000 (paid over a three-year period) to the construction of an electronics laboratory and $2.4 million in annual operating funds. Another $3 million in equipment gifts added to the center's laboratory resources. Because the sponsoring firms have been assiduous in not taking an active role in the administration or in actively guiding research, they could be viewed as a "neutral" third party. A large chunk of the operational monies required to sustain the CIS research program are solicited from the federal government on a contractual basis.

Passive Influence vs Active Influence

Who sets the research agenda? When Erich Bloch, formerly at IBM and currently the NSF director, led the move to create the SRC, he was quick to state that "no federal funding will be solicited." The intention was clear. Industry wanted to run the show, and, indeed in the SRC case it has. Its funds are disbursed to a network of research establishments with the full intention of the SRC controlling the agenda and the tempo.

Being a funder and wanting an active decision-making role can also go wrong. In Massachusetts, the state government, under former Governor Ed King, took the initiative to fund a new microelectronics center in response to successful efforts in North Carolina, California, and Texas. His successor Michael Dukakis, however, viewed the large state investment of $20 million as a means of exerting influence by withholding the state's financial share. What ensued was a damaging battle among corporate and university members, the governor's office, and legislators. The end result was considerable friction, divided allegiances, and a delay that cost the Commonwealth of Massachusetts at least two years in lost time. In the fast-moving, highly competitive world of electronics, two years can be a deadly eternity.

Different attitudes prevailed within the CIS, CIDMAC, and MCNC. In the latter case, the state of North Carolina through its Department of Commerce has provided support without strings or direct involvement. The state wants jobs, jobs that would result from firms being attracted to the vicinity of a world-class research laboratory in electronics. It wants no role in guiding the research, hiring of staff, or determining who will or will not be a corporate participant. The integrity of this role has been achieved so far—and commendably—because visionary governors ensured that shortsighted politics did not hamper the research.

"When we set up the CIS," says George Pake, vice president of research at Xerox, Palo Alto, one of the first to join John Young of Hewlett Packard, Dick DeLauer of TRW, and Robert Noyce of Intel in funding the CIS, "we did it with an explicit goal of not interfering in the academic agenda." The university administers the Center, which was built with corporate donations from twenty firms. The staff, under the leadership of two co-directors, John Linvill and James Meindl, follows its own agenda. But it does, as a matter of course, intend to align its agenda with industry needs. The two sides are working in concert, neither having to strong-arm the other. The original funders do a lot to express their interest but do little to dictate the research agenda. The result is a collegial atmosphere in which researchers from academe and others on leave from industry share projects, reports, and research findings formally through papers or informally in casually arranged meetings. "We wanted to have an arm's-length relationship with faculty," stresses George Pake. "Each company makes an annual contribution of $120,000—this is worth $1 million when it's without strings."

Hewlett Packard's industry representative to the CIS, Dr. Zvonko Faranzic, explained the arm's-length relationship this way. "My instruction is to try and maximize the benefit for the university....This will come back to industry. My IBM colleague has the same instruction. We are not trying to influence the research. But we do suggest problems that we face. In this sense, there is indirect influence. They like to see their work be useful. Industry has no powers at CIS. But it can influence by making people aware of problems they could solve. Sponsors don't shy away from this kind of gentle prodding. There aren't any formal ways. No strings attached."

A similar situation prevails at CIDMAC, administered by the engineering department of Purdue University. Of all the consortia studied, CIDMAC is exemplary in finding a comfortable working middle ground between industry and academe. "We just don't do contractual work," says Dean Henry T. Yang, the center's director and Purdue's engineering department dean. "Education of students is key. We feel our job is to increase the talent pool."

Larry Hollingshead, Cincinnati Milacron's on-site representative agrees: "The manpower pool is limited. In that respect CIDMAC is key in creating know-how in automated manufacturing. If you think that's an easy thing for industry to accept," he adds "remember that back at my company some expected CIDMAC to load something onto a truck and deliver it to GM. There's been a change since then in attitudes."

Changing attitudes didn't come automatically, although it did start with a visionary dean, John C. Hancock, who started the ball rolling by inviting industry to consider developing a new center with Purdue. Control Data was his first partner, and things moved from there.

CIDMAC was formally established in 1982. It had four industry partners and an ambitious mission: full integration of automated manufacturing technologies. In simpler terms, that meant getting people, machines, and computers talking to one another and coordinating their actions forwards and backwards along a production line. Companies are in for $1 million a piece to be paid out over a five-year period plus extras as they see fit. Purdue built a special lab for another $500,000. "I've never seen such a fast turnaround as that at Purdue," says Professor Jim Solberg of the six-month idea-to-building turnaround.

Cummins Engine of Columbus, Indiana, is a partner. "We felt that the academic world had drifted far from industry with NASA and NSF as supporters," said Jerry Schlensker, Vice President for Manufacturing at the company. "There had been a long history of university and industry relations in manufacturing. But Sputnik drew them apart. Suddenly there was 'free money' for researchers only loosely tied to a product. No strings attached. They didn't need industry. There was a spin-off to high-tech, but general manufacturing was not driven by that.

"Cutbacks in federal spending and intensified world competition led universities to say 'we have technology to bring to the party, therefore we can do something.' Dean Hancock with Control Data set up the computer-aided design lab. He then took this to a broader base, the mid-West's heavy manufacturing. He invited companies to talk."

Getting rolling took time, a lot more time than was expected. "It took us about one year to relearn to work together. Trust-building," stated Schlensker. "After eight months of talks we were able to clarify their goals and ours. They were different but not opposed." The result was a clearly stated set of expectations and of common purpose between the academics involved and the five corporate participants.

Eventually, through numerous meetings, a CIDMAC mission was defined. It reflected two sets of "desires." These we quote below from a working memorandum:

University researcher expectations and desires:

- create an environment in which to conduct research
- shorten time from concept to use
- gain new knowledge or extend existing knowledge
- develop projects and thesis subjects for students
- contribute/use knowledge and research capability
- have access to industry and physical production
- have resources to conduct research—money/equipment and facilities
- publish information/concepts/research data
- learn industry needs
- engage in projects
  - interesting and exciting
  - allow creativity and blue sky at times
  - allow freedom of thought and direction
  - CIDMAC provides integration and overall coordination rather than just projects

Industry expectations and desires:

- improve productivity and provide tools to maintain competitive edge
- bring more knowledge to bear on problems we (industry) do not know how to solve
- help integrate CAD/CAM/Automation and develop solutions to missing links in the system
- help manage the explosion in new technologies in this field
- provide solutions that remove the drudgery of work by mechanizing repetitious tasks such as analytical calculations, reporting, and those of a physical nature; free up people to do more important and creative things
- provide solutions that are user friendly and totally interactive
- provide training of industrial personnel; involve industry personnel in some generic research
- help industry avoid reinventing the wheel

- help break out of historical ways of doing things; provide a catalyst for new ways
- provide solutions to our type of problems
- be able to justify participation in the CIDMAC program

This list is important, possibly unique. Rarely does one find the interests of both sides so explicitly stated or recorded. The merit of this exercise is in pointing to common ground within which to collaborate. Schlensker's biggest concern was to break old molds. "We didn't want to have the National Science Foundation problem of having to translate research into useful terms. We wanted it to be user friendly." Illustrating the point he mentioned a large NSF grant provided some Purdue researchers to solve warehousing and inventory problems. "They were still in stacker cranes. In industry we were trying to get rid of inventory as a way of doing business. They were going after the wrong thing," said Schlensker. "The work wasn't relevant." Ironically, in 1985, Purdue was the recipient of a five-year, $17 million NSF Engineering Research Center grant to create a Center for Intelligent Manufacturing Systems that capitalized on the practical goals established by CIDMAC.

What we find from the CIDMAC case, and others referred to above, is that active or passive involvement of industry in academe's agenda setting cannot be prejudged as good or bad. If anything, CIDMAC idealizes the potential relationship that can come from industry and academe—even if it took time and considerable patience to reach that point. Both sides were able to pinpoint desires, they were able to craft a joint mission that didn't compromise either side, and they committed to a relationship with a five-to ten-year horizon.

Federal Government In vs Federal Government Out

The federal R&D obligations for 1984 totaled $43 billion dollars (outlays are somewhat less)—or 2.5 times higher than a decade earlier. They rose to $57 billion in 1986. It seems strange, therefore, to think of a research endeavor that might not include federal dollars.

But if one scrutinizes the federal R&D budget, as we did earlier in this book, it turns out that 60 percent or $26 billion, in 1984, and an estimated 68 percent, or $39 billion, in 1986, was defense related. In short, the lion's share is going in increased proportions to noncivilian R&D. Within defense R&D, it becomes evident that very little effort is going into generic research that, by definition, might have greater commercial utility. In 1986, a mere 3 percent, or $800 million, went to basic research. Also, acceptance of federal research dollars, especially those with defense missions, comes quite encumbered. The most onerous strings-attached condition is an increasing effort by the federal government to close its defense research to outside review. The chain reaction in an academic community committed to open research is implosive.

The constraints can quickly clamp down on industry. Thus, the decision to solicit, or not to solicit, federal R&D dollars is increasingly influenced by the growing promimence of the federal defense R&D agenda. "Government motives can be counterproductive," says Dr. Pake of Xerox. "For example, the federal government through the Commerce Department wants U.S. companies to keep closed-mouthed on technology; yet our state government wants us to show off the CIS to one and all."

Companies whose well-being depends on survival in an intensely competitive world market want no part of an increasing catalogue of federal R&D constraints. This in fact is what led the SRC, from its inception, to exclude any federal involvement from its semiconductor research agenda. As a result, pooled SRC-industry money is outspending the federal government semiconductor research budget by almost three to one. Private industry, in effect, has redirected the national R&D agenda in semiconductor research. The SRC funds are used to contract universities to engage in pieces of the research agenda. By early 1984, six leading universities had received about $7 million in SRC research grants; a second tier of twenty-seven universities and colleges received another $5.5 million. The biggest grants of $1.5 million each went to Cornell and Stanford.

There is a second approach to securing federal monies. This is the one-time "line-item" federal appropriation for a consortium. These appropriations are most often tucked into major pieces of legislation through effective lobbying. The results can be significant to universities strapped for funds. One Washington, D.C.-based firm, Cassidy and Associates, Inc., lobbied more than $200 million for about thirty clients over a seven-year period. The down side is that everyone else who didn't get a grant is up in arms. Their argument is that such grants have not been subjected to peer review and that, as a result, the best-suited recipients may be out of the running and the funds skewed to those with most political pull. If money were abundant and the competitive pressures less great, the argument might hold. But as budgets tighten and resources shrink, those with the greatest entrepreneurial know-how may prove to be the winners. Such competitiveness may not be unhealthy—especially in the university world.

A third course is the one the CIS at Stanford followed. Already briefly described earlier, the CIS was created by agreements crafted by the university and its industry partners. It then turned to the federal government for contracts that would allow it to pay for the costs of the research agenda it had settled on. This course greatly diminishes the "front-end" influence the federal government has in determining the research agenda and staffing of a consortium.

A new approach for disbursing federal monies is contained in the NSF's Engineering Research Centers (ERCs) grants. Here federal monies are channeled to industry-university consortia. The main criteria for winning an ERC grant are (1) likelihood of new knowledge generation, (2) improving the U.S. competitive position, (3) linkage to strengthening the educational system, (4) industry participation, and (5) cross-disciplinary research. In May 1985, the first ERC grant winners were announced. They were Columbia University in telecommunications ($20 million); MIT in biochemical engineering ($20 million); the University of California at Santa Barbara for robotics systems ($14 million); the University of Delaware in conjunction with Rutgers University doing research on composites of wood, ceramics, or other materials ($7.5 million); the University of Maryland in collaboration with Harvard University with computer-aided engineering and artificial intelligence ($16 million); and Purdue University, partially self-adjusting manufacturing systems to reduce cost, time, and errors in manufacturing ($17 million). These are hefty sums, although small in relation to the NSF's overall $1 billion plus annual allocations. But the strong emphasis on engineering and the practical agenda of directly linking research to improved competitiveness is novel.

What should be the specific emphasis of the research agenda, and where should the work be executed to achieve the best results? We explore those implications next.

85

Chapter 9

THE AGENDA

If theory were helpful, we would persist in letting inventions accumulate out of basic research programs and hope for a massive fall out of practical technological innovations. But theory may not accommodate the reality of competitors beating at our doors and winning growing chunks of marketshare. This presents a series of conflicts in determining the most appropriate research agenda for a consortium. What should it be and who's going to call the shots?

Pure Research vs Product Goals

"Real research goes far upstream," commented Dr. George Pake, vice president of research at Xerox in Palo Alto. "Only a handful of companies did this well in the United States: AT&T and GE for example. We often think of R&D as linear flow. That's inaccurate. Its helps set long-term views. Consortia reflect this long-term view. Any joint venture between industry and university is fundamentally long range. That's my view. Pharmaceuticals firms put a lot [of money] into R&D but it's mostly testing not pure research. They got caught by DNA research born in academe. They weren't prepared. They could have built their own R&D like Xerox and my program here. Corporate biotech people didn't want to take the long-term view."

Not everyone agrees that consortia need only be committed to longer term research. Indeed, one can categorize consortia on a spectrum running from pure research to narrow product development. At one extreme, one would put the SRC where there is a five- to ten-year commitment to engage in fundamental research. At the other extreme, we would place MEAC, where contracts are written for as short as six months for a delivered product. Carnegie-Mellon's Robotics Institute would fall in between with technology and research deadlines stradling from the long-term to the very short. Or the MCC in Austin, Texas, tends to the longer term. It has four programs. They are software technology, semiconductor packaging, VLSI Computer-Aided Design, and Artificial Intelligence/Knowledge-Based Systems. They have research horizons of 6,7,8, and 10 years, respectively. They intend to deliver a product. The risk, otherwise, is that their twenty industrial sponsors will scream if they do not—but they have a long time horizon to do so.

Some industry-university consortia have multiple goals. The Rochester Optics Institute is a case in point. From New York State's point of view, the agenda is to create jobs for New York. From Rochester University's point of view, the task is pure research. And spectacular pure research is going on—Rochester being only one of two universities in the country that has graduate programs in optics.

Dr. Kenneth Teegarden, director of the Optics Institute, selected his center's projects in consultation with the faculty, whose purpose is pure research. "The main purpose of the Center is basic research, new and classical optics, particularly lasers and new optical materials—holograms," he explains. "The main interest from New York State is economic development and job creation. The main interest of industry is simply to keep in touch with technology that is so new that no one knows what the commercial projects might be." The center currently has a $2 million budget. "We could double or triple that budget except that the people at the University of Rochester are concerned about balance."

Rochester's Laboratory for Laser Energetics (its director is Robert McCrory) also works closely with the Optics Institute. It has the biggest laser in the world, covering the size of several football fields. This represents yet another university-industry consortium. Founded in 1975, its experimentation on lasers did not begin until 1980. A current budget of more than $11 million includes $7.5 million from the Department of

Energy for fusion research to complete work of interest to the Department of Defense. It also receives $500,000 from the state of New York, and an additional $3.5 million from corporate sources and other federal sources. The list of corporations includes GE, Empire State Electric Energy Research Corporation, New York State Energy Research and Development Authority, Northeast Utilities Service Company, Ontario Hydro, and Southern California Edison Company. Spectra Physics and McDonnell Douglas, although not engaged in collaborative research, do participate in subcontracts or joint research.

The Laser Lab was originally set up to induce a fusion process by laser energy rather than by magnetic donuts. It is an example of pure research manifested in "space-age" hardware. Twenty-four giant laser cannons fire green beams of light over several hundred yards and simultaneously focus on a piece of material no larger than the eye of a needle. The purpose is to produce a fusion reaction, thereby having an alternative technology to the huge electron accelerators such as the famed Tokomak hardware. Now it's also discovered that this laser technology is coveted as a weapon in the so-called Star Wars, or SDI, campaign. That means more money. But the bad news here is that it may end the lab's open publication commitment.

There's constant interaction between the laser lab and the Center for Advanced Optical Technology. Steve Jacobs has a joint appointment with both the laser lab and the Institute of Optics. Much of the research that comes out of the Center finds its way into the laser lab. Steve thinks that the Center is a terrific idea. "This is a great educational augmentation. It gets our students out of the books and into the real world."

Long-Term Programs vs Short-Term Programs

Closely related to the issue of pure versus applied research is the time horizon of the different industry-university consortia. We've already touched on this. Obviously, the longer the time horizon, the closer it comes to the university's normal pace of research. Industry, on the other hand, tends to operate more quickly because of competitive pressures.

Dennis G. Hall, professor of optics at Rochester, notes that "One thing I am certain of is that research in many of the high-technology areas is likely to be effective only if sustained for a long time at a substantial level.

89

To me, an investment of a minimum of ten years seems appropriate for any truly new technology. After all, ten years is just the amount of time between the demonstration of the first transistor in 1948 and the demonstration of the first integrated electronic circuit in 1958. The semiconductor laser was first demonstrated in 1962, and it has not yet been perfected to everyone's satisfaction. If the cost of a ten-to twenty-year research and development effort appears unacceptably high for a single company, the cost-sharing feature inherent in a consortium may be the only available alternative.''

Yet, for varied reasons, companies seldom can commit in writing to such long horizons. Most often, the practical solution means shorter time spans. At the Center for Manufacturing Productivity at RPI, contracts are written for deliverable products within twelve to eighteen months. The shortest project was at WPI, for six months, and even then employees of an industry partner claimed they might have gotten the same results at a systems house in six weeks!

But even with long-term programs, the actual funding commitment is often shorter. At Athena, IBM is restricted from signing any contract longer than three years, although it says it will stay longer. (The other partner, DEC, is committed for five years.) At MCC, companies sign up for three years, even though the shortest program announced is for six years. At the Rochester Optics Institute, where as Dr. Hall notes there should be a minimum ten- to twenty-year commitment, the open-ended commitments by founding companies only go for four years, which is the sunset provision set for the matching funds from the New York State legislature.

At first blush, it seemed to us that short, applied contracts would be favored by industry and that long, basic research ones would be preferred by the university. While the latter holds true, the former does not always do so. WPI's MEAC program is striving to extend its time horizons, because industry is complaining that they are not getting the strengths the university has to offer—which is new knowledge that takes longer to create.

"On one level," says Dr. Terry Loucks who is responsible for the Norton Company's participation at WPI, "MEAC works for us because they give us stuff we couldn't do ourselves—like robots that handle 'greenware,' a type of abrasive important to our industry. On a second level, however, level two, it is questionable. Are they identifying new, 'missing' knowledge? I don't think so.''

Regional Agenda vs National Agenda

Behind such efforts as the MCNC or MCC, which focus on research programs of importance to the nation, lie equally important efforts to address regional needs. In those cases, state governments have developed aggressive regional growth programs that are leveraged by the presence of consortia facilities. Thus while we may talk about U.S. competitiveness against the Japanese or others in the Pacific Rim countries, we may obscure the fact that there is competition between regions of the United States that is equally intense. North Carolina exemplifies how a rural region dependent on tobacco and furniture has carefully bootstrapped itself up to become one of the country's leading high-tech centers.

Or, ask anyone from Texas who the competition is. ''Our goal,'' says Arthur ''Skip'' Porter, the director of the Houston Area Research Center (HARC), ''is to make Texas the top world center in advanced technology research. We have to do something. We have to diversify the economy beyond oil and cattle. And we have to be better than MIT or Stanford. And we will be!'' With oil prices down, the pressure is on to ''drill'' in new directions.

Two mid-Atlantic states—New Jersey and New York—have had a huge technology research base. Governor Kean of New Jersey claims that his state is first in the nation in electronics R&D expenditures, with companies such as AT&T (Bell Labs) and RCA, first in pharmaceutical R&D expenditures and high ranking in many others, with firms located near New York City and in and around Princeton's industrial parks.

New York State has been in danger of losing its technology base. RPI, for example, is located in Troy, New York, which is the birthplace of the industrial revolution in America. The Bessemer steel process was invented here. The first heating stoves were produced in Troy. At one time it was thought that since Troy was located at the confluence of the Hudson River and the Erie Canal it might eclipse New York City in importance. Today Troy has hit the bottom of the industrial revolution and is trying, with some signs of success, to get on an upward course to the top of the high-tech revolution.

Becoming a leader in high-technology growth is the goal of New York State's ambitious program. "We aim to make RPI and the New York State capital region the 'Silicon Valley of the Hudson.'" Will they do it? Look at the program, started by Governor Hugh Carey, carried on by his successor Governor Mario Cuomo, and directed by Graham Jones, head of the New York State Science and Technology Foundation. Here are some of the pieces outlined in historical sequence.

In 1978, Governor Hugh Carey initiated the crafting of a statewide high-tech policy. The aim was to retain and attract high-tech firms into New York. One of his first steps was to form a High Technology Advisory Council consisting of 24 members—18 from industry, 2 from unions, 1 from a business association, and 3 presidents from universities. One of the first initiatives by the state legislature was exclusively focused on RPI. Called a "steeple of excellence," the commitment took the form of a $30 million interest-free loan for an integrated electronics building. Funds were made available in 1982.

But, such one-sided lavishness did not go unnoticed in other parts of the state. By mid-1982, the RPI award caused other universities to protest its political favoritism. The result was the creation of a more balanced program called Centers for Advanced Technology (or CATs). A budget of about $500,000 was assigned for each of the selected center to spend on planning during 1982-83.

By September 1983, following recommendations that emerged from planning efforts, the legislature and governor awarded $7 million annually for four years to seven New York universities with Centers for Advanced Technology. The programs areas selected included:

1. computer and information systems at Columbia University,
2. biotechnology in agriculture at Cornell University,
3. telecommunications at Polytechnic Institute of New York,
4. health care instruments and devices at SUNY Buffalo,
5. medical biotechnology at SUNY Stonybrook,
6. computer applications and software engineering at Syracuse University, and
7. advanced optical technology at the University of Rochester.

Of the 7 awards, 2½ went to public universities and 4½ went to private ones. (The one-half is Cornell, where part of the university is still considered as public because of the Land Grant designation.) The funds are appropriated by the legislature, with a four-year sunset provision that runs from late 1983 to late 1987. Budgeted at $1 million per center, the state monies have to be matched one-for-one with industry money. Only in exceptional circumstances is federal money eligible for state matching, since most of the schools already get substantial federal grants ($700 million versus the state's $7 million).

The procedure for selecting the seven Centers of Advanced Technology was ingenious. Proposals were solicited from 38 New York research universities and 240 other four-year and community colleges. This generated nineteen responses —some might label them "demands"—for the $7 million appropriated funds. The STF then engaged the National Academy of Science to join in a peer review to select seven finalists out of the nineteen proposals. Using the NAS as an intermediary defused the prospects of favoritism being suggested by the twelve losers.

The seven projects are subject to annual evaluation. Each project has a separate evaluation team chosen by SFT and consisting of at least two industry scientists and two academic researchers. After three years of activity, three are treated as "spectacular successes" by state planners, three are doing well, and one has been problematic. The latter, threatened with a funding cutoff, underwent a restructuring that has pumped new life into it.

The CATs are administered by the New York State Science and Technology Foundation (STF), which existed before the CATs program but was restructured to fit its needs. Acting as a mini-NSF, it is governed by a board whose members are predominantly from industry. The board is apolitical to the point that members state publicly that they will *quit* the board if it is subjected to political pressures. The STF officially reports to the commissioner of commerce by virtue of his role as chairman of the board. Treated, at first, with benign neglect by Governor Mario Cuomo, who serves ex-officio on the board as required by law, the STF now has his full and public support.

While issues remain, including divisiveness over the inclusion of two more state commissioners (for a total of thirteen) and the issue of what might happen after the election (the program survived the transition from Carey to Cuomo, but then both were Democrats), the fact is that at present the New York State program is being effectively executed and well

93

funded. Cuomo in his State of the State message called the program "enormously successful."

New York's experience suggests that a geographically and technologically balanced regional program, largely insulated from direct political pressure, can be implemented with minimum delay and to maximum advantage. It tells also that components of the program—such as the optics program among others—are of national importance. So too with the MCNC in North Carolina or the MCC in Texas. The regional/national dichotomy need not be mutually exclusive. The synergy works when the partnership is properly executed by government, industry, and academic institutions.

University Based vs Non-University Based

Where to locate a consortium? How to administer it? The choice between a university or an independent research institute as an alternative, while it has a great deal to do with personalities and timing, also has a very practical implication. University-based research is open to all-comers and involves strong commitments to "educate"; the independent institute, on the other hand, can avoid getting bogged down in the educational agenda and more importantly can offer a proprietary control over ideas it helps develop for its partners. The ITI or MCC are such examples. The MCC did locate close to the University of Texas but it does not involve students. The ITI, while sited on University of Michigan grounds, makes only occasional use of students in its projects. Those that do participate are there more in support of a faculty person retained to work at ITI.

Eleven of the fourteen industry-university consortia we studied were linked to, or even housed at, a university. Those that are housed at a university tend to have a stronger emphasis on teaching and students—and from an industry perspective —a leg up on hiring new talent. RPI has one of the most extensive programs involving students directly in the university based research. At its Center for Manufacturing Productivity and Technology Transfer, its associate director Bob Messler explains their two main types of activities: projects and programs. Projects involve short six- to fifteen-month research contract signed with individual companies to produce a specific product. Programs have a longer time horizon. In both, undergraduate and graduate students are deeply involved.

Take the project idea for example. A project team usually exists for twelve months and is composed of a project manager (40-50 percent time), a principle investigator (faculty member—25 percent time), a masters student (full time), and an undergraduate (full time). Undergraduates come in and out of the program and have significant responsibility for its eventual success. One of them commented: "You know, it wasn't that the high-ranking scientist from Boeing took me out to lunch and paid for my meal. It was that he was really interested in my ideas on how to automate the assembly of aircraft like the 747. He really listened to me. That's a great feeling!"

MEAC at WPI also has an extensive program to involve students in their activities. As part of the graduation requirement, all undergraduates have to write a thesis on the social impacts of technology, as well as have significant experience in industry. As a result, "WPI students are great," says Gary Newhall at General Motors. "You can hire them and they go to work without any retraining or extensive on-the-job apprenticeship."

Such experiences explain why numerous companies are interested in supporting university-based consortia. The payoff of better trained or educated graduates is often sufficient to warrant the investment; the creation of new knowledge, even under open scrutiny to competitors, offers added return that can be leveraged if the corporate partner has a "first look" at what's going on. If proprietary control over research is important, working outside the university is the obvious alternative.

Public Domain vs Proprietary

Who will own the results of consortia work? This question is the cause of more pain, confusion, and strain than any other. Egos, possible windfalls, institutional reputations, academic careers, industry investment, and public reputations are all intertwined. The issue is money. How it is resolved directly affects the speed with which technology enters the marketplace.

There is no clear resolution to the question of who should own the technologies that come out of collaborative R&D. While patents, copyrights, and licensing rights are the ultimate means of control, ownership or control can take varied forms.

The CIS offers one example. "Consortia put us on new ground," says Dr. George Pake of Xerox. "When several companies came together, problems occurred over *patent policy*. These new technologies (software and chips) created a big question—a big muddle—about ownership and identification of it. Patent protection doesn't work that well. The smell of money has modified the academic approach to throwing results into the public domain. This was much more complicated than I thought. . . . I did not anticipate the delays here.

"On the patent issue," added Pake, "I thought the faculty were too grasping. They were shifting their concerns. Individual motives prevailed over shared ones. Individual professors shook my altruism about academics. Companies started involving their legal departments. One danger was that we'd have to pay royalties. We avoided that."

Stanford University's position was quite different. James Gibbons, who represented the university's interests, recalled the companies' first position being 'We want exclusive rights to anything that's invented in CIS.' "Stanford's point of view was, 'You're putting up a building, but almost everything that goes on in it is paid for with federal money.' " The companies' worst-case scenario was a professor who invented something at CIS and then went out, patented it, and licensed the patent to a competitor.

The debate at Stanford and among corporate partners took time to resolve. New ground had to be broken in forging an "ownership agreement" acceptable to all. The CIS finally settled on a formula that one of the industry representatives calls "a masterpiece of law." President Donald Kennedy of Stanford summarized the meaning of the final document by saying, "this is an experiment, after all."

The CIS treats its industry monies as contributions to a fund and not a contract for services. Any work supported by this fund is considered public domain through prompt publication. On the other hand, if an industry representative invents something while working at the CIS, it is judged to be the property of the company for whom that person works. If, in a third formulation, the invention is the joint effort of a faculty member and an industry representative, the rights belong to the university with the company getting royalties and access to the invention. (See Appendix C for a sample agreement.) One might call this the university-driven formula.

There are others ways of finding ownership harmony. In this case it is industry-driven. At Carnegie Mellon's Robotics Institute, companies enter into contractual agreements for services. Patents are covered by a two-sided formula. If an invention is jointly created by a team that includes a company's employees and CMU people or by the company's employees alone while at CMU, rights belong to the company involved. If the company licenses those patents it pays CMU a percent of the royalties. Any invention created solely by CMU employees on a company-financed project belongs to CMU with the sponsor(s) getting nonexclusive rights to it. Affiliates of the Institute get free nonexclusive rights to any patents obtained by CMU from projects supported in whole or in part by funds from the Industrial Affiliates Program. (See Appendix D for a sample agreement.)

At Purdue's CIDMAC, the ownership rules take a different turn. One reason is that companies are not contracting for the development of a specific product that will "walk out of the door." The work is treated as generic research and the contractual relationship between university and company is drafted in relatively loose terms. All foreign and U.S. rights from CIDMAC inventions belong to the university through the Purdue Research Foundation. Company sponsors—or their licensees world-wide—have the right to use patents, copyrights and other intellectual properties on a nonexclusive unrestricted worldwide basis. Royalties are negotiated with the university. Faculty participants of CIDMAC, however, cannot publish or use confidential case data without authorization. "This partnership is based on trust," says Jerry Schlensker of Cummins Engine, "Purdue could go out and sell rights to our competitors. Indeed Cummins could go out and sell them to others. The bottom line, though is selling products not technology."

In yet another variation, the Indiana Corporation for Science & Technology illustrates the problem of a funding group wanting control over patent and commercial rights against the will of universities such as Purdue. Alden McLellan, CST's first president, held out for ownership of inventions. "I had a fear that if we left them to universities, they'd just bury them. The CST ownership idea got industry support because companies felt they could have access to them. Universities didn't like that. The two biggest were against it. Ely Lilly locked horns with them and swapped versions. The resolution was to give universities the ownership but not the licensing right. CST kept that. The right to license is negotiated project by project. If a project goes big we want to be paid back.''

Another illustration of the mechanics involved in manipulating proprietary rights comes from a project that was awarded one of the larger grants made by the CST $930,000. The recipient was the CTS Corporation (not to be confused with the CST) in concert with Notre Dame University. Craig N. Ernsberger, project engineer for the CTS Corporation, a private high-tech firm, described the process he went through.

> Notre Dame approached us on our surface analysis capabilities. At the same time I was preparing a proposal on the subject. I got to Dr. Albert Miller [professor at Notre Dame] up there and we agreed there was overlap. We thought of setting up a fellowship for a grad student...and I became the 'grad.' That phase of work is now over.
>
> Dr. Miller and I generated a proposal to CST. And it was accepted. CTS Corporation develops and maintains the patents. CST, on the other hand, has the option to sub-license in the event CTS Corporation no longer uses the patent or the contract is terminated. Notre Dame has no patent rights but does get to do basic research and to leverage funds into a larger program. Notre Dame has a subcontract through which we get Dr. Miller's expertise and some capital equipment. New equipment purchased goes to CTS but Notre Dame students have access to it. The CST grant is a 'contingency loan.' We have to pay back through royalties the amount borrowed.
>
> We will encourage other companies to participate in this research. Our game plan would be to hold a symposium to open research on plasma processing—our gain would be a jump in time over the next company. We want others to be involved in order to overcome market inertia. All this wouldn't have happened without CST. The risk is necessarily higher than most projects. But it took an *equipment intensive step*. To me its seed money to prove we're beyond the idea stage.

Commenting on the ownership problem, McLellan sees university recalcitrance as somewhat illusory. ''The point of resistance on ownership is in university administrations. They feel they are giving up something that affects their 'image.' It's not the matter of money that is key.''

He may be right. Most universities are ill equipped or not experienced enough to move a patent into the marketplace aggressively—and few do it effectively enough to leverage huge financial rewards. In its Center for Interactive Computer Graphics, RPI owns the software that is developed. It is made available to all thirty eight participating companies, but RPI owns it. In fact, they even market and sell one piece of software, but they are not well set up to do this, so don't foresee earning big bucks in this area. But according to Mary Johnson, "Every month I talk with our legal advisors in the university contract office who keep telling me we have to make this option more viable. Suppose we developed the next Lotus 1-2-3!"

More extreme, on the subject of retaining proprietary control, are the cases in which the consortium is structured to protect clients proprietary rights. The ITI in Michigan is an example. Originally designed to be a consortium of numerous small companies, it settled into being a contract research institute. "We're built to deal with proprietary information," says its director Jerome Smith. "A university would allow freer inquiry but to many companies that just isn't desired. This becomes truer and truer the closer you come to applications." The ITI, although located on the grounds of the University of Michigan, is legally and administratively independent. This allows it to engage in contractual relationships with corporate clients with greater assurance of protecting proprietary information.

At MIT, the patent issue has an unusual twist. In contrast to the case at CMU, MIT, not IBM or DEC, owns the rights to any software developed. The issue for MIT is to what extent the faculty (and students) who develop the software should share in any potential royalties. The matter is unresolved.

There are varied other resolutions to the patent and ownership issue. Those described above offer a glimpse into the conflicting interests and wide-ranging solutions. One way to sum up the patent issue is by quoting Rick Parmelee, IBM's representative at Project Athena. "If we gave Faulkner a typewriter, we wouldn't expect royalties from his book!"

Interdisciplinary vs Narrow Disciplinary Focus

When establishing a consortium, particularly in a university, should the founders do so within an existing department or should they create new entities that incorporate several departments in implementing a research agenda? One of the more significant features of industry-university consortia is the interdisciplinary focus of their work—or, in other words, integrating disciplines to solve problems. The reason for this is that narrowly proscribed departmental disciplines cannot respond to technologically complex problems.

At RPI, not only are the programs interdisciplinary—involving at least the departments of materials, mechanical engineering, electrical engineering, computer systems engineering, physics, computer science, and chemistry—but the new Center for Industrial Innovation building will physically interweave the offices and laboratories of people from each of these disciplines.

This same interdisciplinary focus was true in one form or another at every consortium we studied. Perhaps the most interdisciplinary was Project Athena at MIT. Due to the nature of the project, it involved almost every department at the Institute.

David Lampe, for example, is in the English composition department. He is collaborating with Pat Winston, head of the artificial intelligence department, to create an expert system that teaches students how to improve their writing—a system that will serve as a tutor, causing the user to ask questions about the process of writing. David Dobrin oversees the project and works closely with IBM's representative on campus, Rick Parmelee. There's Dave Epstein, who is using the system to create music. He works with a piano keyboard and synthesizer on the Athena computer screen. Or there's Nan Freedlander who specializes in transportation economics and computer applications to social science.

At WPI, the MEAC consortium had a profound effect on the mechanical engineering department. For many years, perhaps too many, mechanical engineering had become rusty, yet it still dominated the school's curriculum up through the 1960s. But the advent of MEAC with its focus on electrical engineering and computer science has transformed the mechanical engineering division, bringing it up to date and integrating it with electrical methods. "Students were voting 'pro e/e' with their feet,'' one professor recounted. Robots and electronics were getting the enrollments. Mechanical engineering saw it happening at its expense, and its faculty quickly learned that they had to adapt and combine forces with electrical engineers.

At Stanford's CIS, one of the primary goals is to integrate the work of hardware and software people. In practice, this means considerable effort to get the electrical engineers to work with computer sciences—two groups that are not normally integrated at Stanford. The difficulty is understood by discovering that the electrical people fall under the jurisdiction of the engineering department and the computer science ones fall under that of the humanities and sciences department. This means two cultures with different reward systems, different collections of students, and different perspectives on how to tackle or analyze problems. Blending them into one, although obvious in relation to problems that need solving, is far from obvious when it comes to the mechanics. Stanford not only took on substantive problems requiring their cooperation but also housed the interdisciplinary team in its own new building, the CIS. Physical proximity is vital in engendering intellectual contact.

When we discuss interdisciplinary work, we may think first of the university. But it holds true for industry as well. John Wilson notes: ''We had a need in Cincinnati Milacron for excellence. We realized that we were becoming a multidisciplinary industry. So we expanded our contacts in many different places. We've had to think about how far we reach out regionally. It's more difficult to actually have people on the university campus. But when they're there, you get more leverage. We have a new discipline coming in in polymers and advanced composites. There's center of excellence coming forward in Delaware so we'll go there.'' The Delaware Center is also multidisciplinary. It recently received a large grant from the National Science Foundation.

But there is another dimension—a missing one—to the challenge of integrating disciplines around technological problems. Inventing better ways of managing the use of technology, particularly process technologies, is a part of a big picture largely overlooked by U.S. business and business schools. One would think, therefore, that many consortia would make this a primary concern, given the strong emphasis on technology transfer and on economic productivity. Yet they do not, and this, for the moment, is a serious oversight. On the campus, at least, the engineering

101

and business schools are proverbially miles apart. In reality, they should be intimately intertwined. Academics will rationalize the division with arguments about accreditation, having to meet standards or problems of tenure. At Boston University, efforts are being made to invent joint degrees administered by autonomous centers with borrowed departmental faculty. Other campuses, such as MIT, are experimenting with programs in technology management. Dartmouth College is searching for ways to link its Thayer School of Engineering and Tuck School of Business whose facilities physically adjoin.

"The partner missing who has the biggest effect on how industry organizes is the business schools," says Terry Loucks, of the Norton Company. "I find them glaringly absent in the R&D consortia if linking them is one of the hidden objectives. Recently in a NSF Engineering Research Center proposal [Loucks sits on a final review committee], one of the unsuccessful proposals was from a 'namebrand' school who literally included their business school in their proposal as being an important element. That's because many times engineers can't do a ten-year discounted cash flow or ROI that might overcome management hurdles. At the same time, people we're graduating from these business schools are still moving up faster than technical people—not that that's bad—it's just that they are oblivious to R&D management." The "management gap" calls for a solution and for reconsideration of the interdisciplinary qualities of consortia programs.

Beyond the general matter of defining what goes into setting an appropriate agenda is the question of leadership and image. The two are related ingredients vital to the success of R&D consortia and to maintaining the vitality of the new alliance.

Chapter 10

LEADERSHIP

Leadership is a sine qua non of any human endeavor. Its manifestation can take many different forms, some of which are explored in this chapter. One variation is the coupling of physical space to an understanding of the leadership role. The connection is more obvious, as we will find out, if one's perception of leadership also means affecting behavior of participants or the public image of something as abstract as a *consortium*. Providing a physical home with its own identity—or image—is a potent if not subtle method of influence. For example, proper architectural design and siting can invite interactions between people through intelligent manipulation of spaces.

Strong Leadership vs Diffuse Leadership

One of the first findings is that innovative leadership can emerge from an array of places: a professor with a singleminded mission (Professor Robert Hexter and the Minnesota Center for Microelectronics and Information Services (MEIS) at the University of Minnesota), a dean of engineering (John Hancock at Indiana), a university president (Dr. Richard Cyert at Carnegie-Mellon, or Edmund Cranch at WPI), a governor (Hunt in North Carolina, Milliken in Michigan, or Cuomo in New York), and corporate executives (Erich Bloch of IBM, or William

Norris of Control Data, or John Young of Hewlett-Packard). In one case, after the founding of the Industrial Technology Institute in Michigan, new leadership came from a foundation. The Kellogg Foundation based in Battle Creek decided to turn its interests away from national issues and inward to its home state. Its backing of the state-created ITI with multimillion-dollar funding was significant because it preceded any effort by the "big three" auto makers, the logical leaders in getting the ITI off the ground, to take the lead. Kellogg committed additional large resources to other initiatives in the state.

Can an R&D consortium survive and thrive without strong leadership? No. Can it survive with diffuse leadership? Probably not. This conclusion comes in part from observing the trial and error evolution of several consortia. One suffered from too many "chefs," another from committee leadership, and a third from a failure to anticipate day-to-day management problems.

The too many "chefs" problem was at the Massachusetts Electronics Center (MEC), a project of the Massachusetts Technology Park Corporation. A creature of the legislature, it got mired in the conflicting agendas of an agglomeration of partners. A dominant leader with a clear and persuasive vision never emerged. One effect was to delay its implementation, although it eventually reached the stage of breaking ground on permanent facilities and distributing equipment resources to its university members, some of whom complained that the free equipment was not optimally suited to the intended research tasks.

One almost needs an adding machine to count all those who had a hand in leading the MEC into being: two governors, state legislators, two succeeding secretaries of economic affairs, seven universities and their presidents and deans of engineering, a dozen influential corporate CEOs and company founders, and a beleaguered MEC president. It was a case of too many chefs trying to make a delicate soufflé. Diffuse leadership and competing intentions do not mix. They deflate. And in Massachusetts, at least, it allows divisive politics, the state sport, to thrive.

There's another kind of diffusion of leadership: committee directorates. It is problematic and perhaps more common. This kind was in evidence at the University of Minnesota's corporate-funded MEIS during its germinal years. How, for example, does one invite research proposals and then make decision on funding allocations? Early in its life, the MEIS counted on a committee of professors for suggestions. And they came up with many: Their own. "We had twenty professors and twenty-one conflicting proposals for funding," said Professor Robert Hexter of the MEIS. Each faculty person proposed a pet personal agenda. This method fell far short of drawing the most qualified projects to the fore. The committee was soon abandoned in favor of a more centrally managed decision-making process in which corporate sponsors had a stronger say.

Purdue's CIDMAC encountered its own leadership learning curve. "We found," Jerry Schlensker recounted, "the structure wasn't working. The policy and technical committees were setting direction but they weren't managing the research. The old way with an NSF grant meant a professor and his project. We wanted a process that would guide the research along." A new technical coordinating committee was created to review research work in process. This provides better control by allowing university and industry partners to oversee ongoing work together. Since its creation, research has stayed on track.

Part of the leadership question is resolved in building the proper structure to carry out a consortium's activities. An example of a highly centralized decision-making process is the Corporation for Science and Technology in Indianapolis. Founded in 1982, the CST is a not-for-profit corporation with a 25-person board that includes politicians (3), university presidents (8), companies (6), unions (1), and six other public and nonprofit agencies or institutions (6). The board embodies the "consortium," or partnership—the diffuse part of the structure. Monies supplied in two-year doses by the legislature are used, in turn, to contract out new technology initiatives that will produce jobs for Indiana, provide technological counsel and advice, and offer financial and business counseling. The latter is an important service, particularly so because many small companies or potential start-ups are involved in the CST.

Perhaps because of traditions of which Indianians are proud, politics played little role in skewing the process. This allowed a grant review system to be devised that inhibits political interference or pressure. As Alden McLellan, CST's first president, described it, the "CST is separate from government. I had direct requests from politicians, but I channeled them through the process." The process was designed to moved swiftly. Grant proposals are turned around from receipt to final yes/no decisions in three months without reviewers knowing who the applicant is. "The first $3 million was hard to give away," recalled Alden. "We had to walk into research rooms looking for projects of commercial value. Opening lines of communication is a primary function of CST."

The first filter is a network of sixteen committees through which proposals are submitted for consideration. Each committee oversees a particular technology. A total of 500 volunteer specialists participate as committee members, each group a minicomposite of the cross-section of consortium partners. "These people," says current president John D. Hague, "are selected without regard for political preference and serve to ensure that the decisions are based upon business and technological information and are not driven in any way by political influence."

Proposals filtered by these committees are submitted for a yes/no vote by the president and a small review group. The yes proposals go simultaneously to a technical committee for outside review by two or three experts and to a funding committee. If the request is for $100,000 or less, the decision can be made there. For higher amounts, it goes to the executive committee and then to the full board. In 1984, the process led to $11,500,000 in grants: 43 percent to university and industry joint ventures, 29 percent to universities, 17 percent to industry, and 11 percent to entrepreneurs. "In proposals," said Hague "we look for ties to the private sector." Fifty-seven grants were authorized in 1985; twice as many as a year before. By 1986, a cumulative total of $31 million in disbursements had been made.

Leadership in the CST's case comes from an activist president and from a network of committees with clearly delegated authority. Take away the leadership or the clear structure, and the process falls apart rapidly.

Physical Identity vs No Physical Identity

Following a commentary on leadership with a discussion about buildings may seem dissonant. There is, however, a direct connection. Each symbolize the image and ideals of their enterprises. In the first instance it is done by individuals who personify the goals and qualities of a program; in the second instance it is a building that provides a physical manifestation of the same program's goals and ambitions.

Symbolism and stability are vital parts of an institution's image. RPI knew this well when it built a new technology center. With the center, a new building was put under construction. According to Christopher Le Maistre, director of the Center for Industrial Innovation, which will be housed in the new building, the architectural design is dramatically and intentionally symbolic. Presently scheduled for completion in November 1986, the building is not only located in the center of the campus but it purposely forms the "gateway" to the campus. "No one will be able to ignore the statement it makes," says Le Maistre. "All the other RPI buildings are in buff brick color, reminiscent of the old American industrial era which was born in Troy. This new building is in high-tech white with bright red trim. More importantly, it physically integrates the ten different disciplines that work on the three different centers by physically interweaving their laboratories one into the other."

Further, he adds, "We purposely disrupted life on campus by constructing a building right at the gateway. Everyone has to take notice of the new RPI. *We are changing the culture of the established university.*" [Authors' emphasis.]

Because R&D consortia are crafting a new image of technology as a driving force, image and aura are important features. Thus a decision to build, or not to build, is linked to the question of how consortia should be tangibly manifested. Should the decision be to build, the architectural interpretation of the building acquires new importance: Should the effect be discreet? Should it be a public demonstration of an ambition? Should it seek to alter perceptions?

Purdue University, located in rural West Lafayette, Indiana, had (until 1984) the largest engineering department in the United States. It is now fourth with 6,402 enrollments and second in degrees granted. Despite its size, engineering wasn't considered the "sexiest" or "best playing field" for majors. As a result, many of the campus stars chose other fields such as law, medicine, or business school. But when the University decided to build a manufacturing lab for CIDMAC, there was an immediate reaction from students.

"We wanted the best labs," said Larry Hollingshead of Cincinnati Milacron, a consortium member. "This attracted students overnight. And a surprising number of women. We're getting the best students on campus." One of the primary reasons is visual impact of the new lab. An experimental automated production line was created behind a modern glass facade in a newly constructed building wing. Mechanical parts are brightly painted. It has an inviting, hands-on appearance. It represents the reality of the work going on and the relationship of this work to computer technologies. All this contributed to a feeling that CIDMAC was a "big deal" on campus. Professor James Solberg put it this way: "The lab—and the speed with which it was put up—signaled university-wide that this was important."

Similar effects were achieved at Stanford when the CIS opened its new laboratory building early in 1985. Not only does its stylish unique design by architects Erlich-Rominger provide it with physical identity, but through intelligent layout of interior spaces a far more important goal is achieved. Open floor layouts and shared spaces in the building symbolize the explicit goal of avoiding departmentalizing CIS faculty.

"The real issue," says Richard Reis, assistant director of the CIS, "is faculty interaction. Are the computer science people really involved? Was electrical engineering dominating? Two years ago there was a real question about this. Computer science people were asking whether they would have space or even projects to work on." With one-half of the CIS faculty housed in the building, or about thirty-five people plus industry representatives, the hope is that proximity will eliminate barriers between disciplines. "The building is key in that regard," says Reis. "It makes it easier for them to work together."

Hopes the CIS has for its new home are shared by the MCNC, which is 3,000 miles away in North Carolina. It was there, prior to the building of the CIS, that architects O'Brien/Atkins Associates created a micro-electronics center that is distinctly similar in aspiration as the CIS's. The MCNC laboratory is designed to stimulate interaction between staff, researchers, and industry representatives. Sitting areas are handily located, people and their work are visible, and opportunities for formal or informal exchange are maximized. Walking through the plush open corridors and past the glassed-in, super-high-tech, class-1 clean room, a visitor is struck by the relaxed and open atmosphere. It becomes evident that good design and architecture can play a vital role in stimulating human interaction. This in turn can lead to greater integration between disciplines, an essential condition for these consortia to carry out their complex technological assignments.

It should hardly be suprising that layouts and designs of physical space intimately affects people's actions. Indeed, Winston Churchill often credited the unique style of British democracy to the design of its parliamentary debating chambers. Facing one another, opposition parties had ample opportunities to interact by cross-examining one another in direct exchanges—heckling became a finely crafted political tool in this environment. The converse is recalled in the disastrous experiences of people required to live in public housing projects such as Pruitt-Igo in St. Louis. Designs of space were so antisocial that the whole project finally was dynamited by the government and cleared.

Proximity and direct contact between researchers and their industrial peers is one characteristic common to successful research and development that good design and architecture can address. But one, also, has to account for the geographic proximity of people. Silicon Valley's entrepreneurial success is often attributed to the closeness of so many bright, restless, and innovative technologists. This is often described as a "critical mass" of creative energy. And it is just this that many consortia seek to create in order to overcome the barrier of dispersed geographic sites.

In Massachusetts, home of the famed Route 128 high-tech beltway and the more recent explosion of artificial intelligence and biotech companies adjacent to MIT in Cambridge, it was ironic that the obvious advantages of geographic proximity got subverted by politics. The MEC, created by an act of the legislature, was intended as a laboratory where the making or process engineering of semiconductors could be taught. Where the MEC would be located was a vital ingredient in attracting a willing audience of teachers and learners from businesses and universities. The importance of access was never considered by Governor Michael Dukakis, who soon after his election in 1982 fought to have the MEC located in a depressed small town removed from the mainstream of electronics activity. Although economic development was the commendable goal, returning favors for political support was the primary motive. Many industry and university leaders were incensed at the governor's failure to understand that politics and technological creativity have little in common. A damaging political battle ensued. Industry leaders won out ultimately, but their ranks were divided.

109

But where Massachusetts suffered from an unfortunate case of political myopia, North Carolina applied its political instincts to more visionary goals. Geography was hardly an ally to North Carolina. Its cities are small, and even the highly touted Research Triangle park sits at the core of a three-town metro area of a mere 400,000 people. There just wasn't any way to duplicate the critical proximity or density of skilled people characteristics of Silicon Valley or Route 128.

One of the questions asked in North Carolina was how to overcome geography. What do you do when your principal microelectronics research partners are 175 miles apart? They included half a dozen industry members, a research laboratory (MCNC), five universities, and a research institute. To James Dykes, vice president and general manager of GE's Semiconductor Division, the ideal is "having people see the need and results up close. This motivates people to work harder. Proximity is critical."

This feeling is echoed by others. Dr. Vernon Chi of the University of North Carolina worked on a Communications Committee chaired by Norm Vogel of IBM. Its goal was to devise a solution to the dispersed geography problem. "Our pious hope," said Chi, "was to be competing at the level of Silicon Valley. They have a close-knit geographic network of schools and a critical mass of technology researchers. Numbers and proximity are key."

Fred Brooks, then chairman of the computer science department of the University of North Carolina, provided the MCNC and its communications committee with the vision. He liked to say that "collaborations don't start long distance but they can happen and persist long distance." He insisted on achieving a system that allowed a one-to-one Socratic method to thrive. The committee invented its own buzzword for Brooks' ambition: *virtual proximity*. "A rich communication system can create this," said Vernon Chi. "It has to allow substance to flow. And it has to be able to transmit our own 'persona' easily. You need to be able to brainstorm directly in a conference setting. It should be no more difficult than running downstairs in your own building."

The key to all this, the committee decided, was high-speed, wide-band digital links and two-way, full-image, real-time hook-ups. The committee designed a 175-mile microwave network linking seven primary locations. The state provided $6.5 million to construct the system that in the

MCNC's words "consists of two interactive, full motion, color television channels and a 12-million-bit-per-second data circuit." Once in operation, the network created a new challenge: scheduling. Demand is so high that not everyone can get access when they want it. Another problem is working out what the system's operating costs actually are.

To MCNC planners, however, the first big step is achieved of bringing the concept of shared resources to a reality. "Our goal," says MCNC president Don Beilman, "is to leverage ourselves through the communication tie-up to universities. This, coupled with industry people we bring in, means that we are creating a hybrid environment. Remember that our job is not profit but technology access with state funding support. We're an experiment."

R&D consortia are experiments, indeed. No two are alike in responding to the complexity of actors, motives, and unique regional circumstances that underlie their creation. Despite this dissimilarity, in Part IV we take a closer look at the workings of a single consortium, the Microelectronic and Computer Technology Corporation—the MCC—in Austin, Texas. Neither typical, nor yet a proven success or failure, the MCC is a case study of big bucks and even bigger hopes at work in Austin, Texas.

Part IV
A CASE STUDY

Chapter 11

MCC:
HIGH STAKES FOR
HIGH TECH

The idea wasn't born in Texas. It came from William Norris, founder and chairman of Control Data Corporation in Minneapolis, Minnesota. A mercurial and far-sighted leader, he cited the Japanese Fifth Generation Computer project as his major reason for his developing the original concept of the MCC. "We have seen the U.S. semiconductor industry's preeminent position in semiconductor memories eroded in a few short years," he said in 1982. "And, the Japanese announced their intent to continue their market momentum in microelectronics while they mount a parallel effort to become the world's leader in computing by the end of the decade."[*]

The Microelectronics and Computer Technology Corporation (MCC), has been in the news since the day it was born. In 1983, with great fanfare, it caused cities and states nationwide to engage in a feverish competition to attract the MCC to their respective folds. Intensive wooing by political, academic, and industrial figures in Texas won the prize for Austin, based on existing plans for investment in complementary research

[*]News Release, "Cooperative Microelectronics R&D Venture Incorporated" (Minneapolis: Control Data Corporation, August 25, 1982).

programs at the oil-rich University of Texas at Austin and Texas A&M. By 1985, MCC was in the news again. Proposed cutbacks in the University of Texas budget provoked MCC's director, Admiral Bobby Ray Inman to say "If we were making the site selection in the spring of 1985 instead of the spring of 1983, I would have to think very carefully about whether I would recommend coming to Texas." Some called it an effective ploy to get the cutbacks to be reversed. They were.

Funds are flowing and the MCC is entrenched for the long haul. But placing bets about the eventual success or failure of MCC is risky. It is so new, different, and on such a grand scale, that it naturally has its critics. "It'll never work," goes one reaction. "It's got too many competing companies, each of whom have overinvested in the project." On the other hand, MCC has grown rapidly, significantly exceeding its initial target of hiring 220 professionals, and it just might make a major breakthrough toward a U.S. Fifth Generation computer. Its full staff totaled 405 by early 1986.

A closer look at this unique consortium illustrates the variety of issues we have been discussing under mechanics and motives. Officially, MCC is not an industry-university partnership at all. It is a private, profit-making company. There are no formal ties to any university, although it is located on lands owned by the University of Texas; nor is there any link to the state government despite Governor Mark White's and San Antonio Mayor Henry Cisneros' aggressive leadership that helped bring MCC to Texas; neither does the federal government play a role even though MCC chairman and president Bobby Ray Inman is a retired admiral and former deputy director of the CIA.

Nonetheless, despite these paradoxical qualities, MCC acts as if it were a partnership similar to the others described in this report but with some major differences in approach and emphasis. An examination of these differences reveals a lot about the partnership concept and at the same time provides yet another strategic alternative that is likely to be duplicated by others in the immediate future.

The Shareholders

As of January 1986, twenty-one companies form the membership of the MCC.* Some of them, like Lockheed and Control Data, are large companies. Others like Advanced Micro Devices are relatively small. But for the most part, these are a group of mid-sized corporations that banded together to do advanced research in response to the Japanese challenge.

There are of course other reasons why this particular group of companies have joined forces. IBM looms large among these. Being able to compete against the formidable IBM research budget was never the galvanizing force that crystalized MCC, nor do its officers dwell on this aspect of MCC's existence. But why isn't IBM a shareholder? "You'd best ask IBM," remarks Bill Stotesbery, a chief assistant to Inman and the man responsible for handling public relations. Perhaps they were concerned they would have to share their own research with competitors, perhaps they felt their investment in the Semiconductor Research Corporation was enough in joint research. Grouping twenty-one medium-sized companies into a $50 to $100 million research consortium is a good start at playing in IBM's league.

Antitrust questions figured prominently in the formation of MCC, and Stotesbery notes that the fear of antitrust may have been another reason why IBM did not become an MCC shareholder. The question, of course, was whether collaboration in research would constitute collusion that could be deemed illegal under existing U.S. antitrust laws. "The Justice Department gave us what I would call 'an amber light,'" said Inman. "In essence, they said we could take the first steps and that they would not oppose us. However, they made no guarantees that this action would be exempt from antitrust considerations." In the meantime, in the fall of 1984 and under the prodding of officials in the Department of Commerce and elsewhere, a bill was introduced and subsequently passed in Congress formally recognizing the right to create research consortia—but not exempting them from future antitrust scrutiny. As far as the MCC was concerned, the amber light turned bright green. The bill passed both the

---

*As of June, 1985, the member companies were: Advanced Micro Devices, Allied Corporation, Bellcore, Boeing, BMC Industries, Control Data Corporation, Digital Equipment Corporation, Eastman Kokak Company, Gould Inc., Harris Corporation, Honeywell Inc., Lockheed, 3M, Martin Marietta Corporation, Mostek Corporation, Motorola Inc., National Semiconductor Corporation, NCR Corporation, RCA Corporation, Rockwell International Corporation, Sperry Corporation.

House and the Senate unanimously. Everyone seems to agree that cooperative research is a plus for the nation. Further, as the MCC case illustrates, it may even provide a way for medium-sized and smaller companies to compete in an industry of giants like IBM and AT&T. To the extent this is the case, one could say that instead of reducing competition, the research consortium prevents concentration by preserving and expanding the knowledge base critical to the survival of, with several exceptions, almost a score of medium sized companies.

The notion of "shareholder" figures prominently in the thinking of MCC officers. The twenty-one companies are called "shareholders" because they have to buy one share of MCC stock in order to join. When we asked whether the consortium was showing early signs of success, Bob Rutishauser, vice president for finance and administration, smiled. "The first companies to join paid $100,000 for a share of stock. That was before anyone knew whether we could be a going concern. Now the board has voted to charge $500,000 for a share of stock." Not long after the conversation, the entry price jumped to $1 million.

So by traditional financial criteria, the MCC is a good investment for its shareholders with a stock price that increased tenfold in two and a half years. This is, of course, no more than a casual indicator, since the stock is not bought and sold like shares on the New York Stock Exchange. What it does reflect, however, is how risky it is to launch research on advanced subjects. Venture capitalists expect a premium on the order of a three-to fivefold increase in three to five years for a "normal" company with a marketable product. In the case of long-term research, the curve is far steeper. The fact that the value of MCC stock has increased ten times indicates both how risky the original enterprise was perceived and also how successfully it is now proceeding.

Corporate Research Culture

A major concern for any type of venture like MCC is whether cooperative research can effectively be performed by competing companies. That is, with 40 percent of the researchers formerly employed by companies engaged in head-on competition, what will happen when they are grouped under the same roof? Further, more than one-half (60 percent) of these people at MCC are not direct hires but what are termed "assigned" or "liaison" personnel, which means that their salaries continue to be paid by the home company rather than directly by MCC. Will these people cooperate like scientists or closely guard the flow of information as competitors might?

Interestingly, this begs the intriguing question of the extent to which scientists are willing to cooperate with one another. Most university research, for example, is centered around a single professor and a smaller or larger group of graduate students. Larger projects may involve the joint efforts of several colleagues or even many members of an academic department. But the MCC has nearly 295 scientists, projected to reach around 350, and a total payroll of 405. How do you get this many people to cooperate with one another?

One cut at an answer to this question lies in culture. The MCC is slowly evolving its own culture. At first, the culture was somewhat cool and corporate: three-piece suits, ties, and corporate precision in specifying goals, objectives, and performance. Certainly this style is in evidence among many of the present top officers of MCC. Among the research staff, as one might expect, more informality prevails—although not to the extent one might find at a Stanford or an MIT. "We recently put in a small cafeteria for lunch breaks, and it's been fabulously popular," says Stotesbery. "People come out to meet one another, and trade ideas. A whole new culture is springing up here."

Of course, the move toward a cooperative culture is not the norm in this fast moving electronics industry. Rugged individualism and daring entrepreneurship still are the staples in the world of start-ups and shake-downs. John Rollwagen, the president of Cray Research, declined the offer to join MCC. "We have an entrepreneurial culture at Cray; cooperative research is not our thing." In the same vein, one notes that the list of shareholders does not include the personal computer manufacturers. No Apple, Commodore, Atari or Tandy here. One could speculate that as this segment of the industry matures, PC manufacturers could also team with leading software companies, just as DEC and Sperry, who also happen to manufacture PCs as well as other products, are in the MCC.

Most likely, the culture, like the MCC itself, will be somewhere between the more formal industrial lab and the sometimes chaotically creative university environment. The position midway between industrial research center and university lab is how most of the top officers see the

119

MCC mission. Chief scientist John Pinkston says that it is the time line that distinguishes different types of research. Most industry labs operate on a maximum of five years into the future. Many, of course, are shorter, concentrating their attention on refining an existing product over the next month or perhaps a year. At the other extreme, there are special research labs that have a time horizon of a decade or more. In this category would be Bell Labs, perhaps some of IBM's work, and certain Defense Department projects (those referred to as "6.1" research) as well as the programs that DARPA funds. The MCC, in contrast, falls between pure and applied research. Its four major research areas have time horizons of 6, 7, 8, and 10 years.

The greatest dose of internal competitiveness comes less at the researcher level than on the technical advisory committee and to some extent on the board of directors. The tug and pull that influences the research direction comes from the industry scientists. They know well that, over the three-year minimum participation period, their company has invested anywhere from perhaps $2 million at the low end to $10 to $15 million at the high end. This is a substantial financial commitment. Although the size of investment varies according to whether the company is in one, two, or perhaps all of the research programs, this is nonetheless an investment of sufficient size that "writing it off" as a failure would cause sleepless nights. So the industry scientists on the technical advisory board push hard to get research relevant to their own needs. Of course it can be argued, as MCC officers do, that this is highly leveraged knowledge that the companies are investing in. A $2 to $10 million investment is bringing back $30 to $50 million worth of research results.

The real measure of success to date are MCC's people and their ability to work as a team. In January 1984, there were only 20 people on the payroll. Ten months later there were 217. "I had hoped to reach that figure by the end of the year, but progress in attracting top talent to Austin has been excellent," says Bobby Inman. Two years later it was up to 295. Is it top talent, or is this a skilled top spokesman's persuasiveness at work?

Seven out of ten professionals are engaged in research work as opposed to administration or support services. Of the research staff in 1984, 44 percent had Ph.D.'s, 24 percent had master's degrees, and 28 percent had bachelor's. About 20 to 25 percent of these people come directly from universities, according to George Black, the vice president for human resources. The rest come from industry, and a few, like Chief Scientist John Pinkston, come from government. Pinkston, for example, spent the past seventeen years with the National Security Agency before making the switch to an industrial environment. With degrees from Princeton and MIT, Pinkston notes that "the culture shock of switching from the NSA to an industry environment was less than I expected."

The Research Agenda

Presently, there are four programs—or seven, depending how they are counted. These are software technology, semiconductor packaging, VLSI Computer-Aided Design (CAD), Artificial Intelligence (AI)/Knowledge-based systems, data-base architectures, human factors technology, and parallel processing. The last four are all part of the "advanced computer architecture" area, which is the largest program. This research agenda was basically set during the founding of MCC by corporate executives.

The agenda-setting process is as follows. The program directors, of whom there are currently seven, submit proposals for new ideas. Five of the current seven are recently hired directly from industry—Laszlo Belady from IBM, Barry Whalen from TRW, John Hanne from Texas Instruments and Osborne, Eugene Lowenthal from Intel, and Raymond Allard from CDC. The two others are Woodrow Bledsoe from the University of Texas and Stephen Lundstrom from Stanford University. An executive committee of Inman, Pinkston, and Smidt (vice president for plans and programs, formerly a business strategist for Sperry) then reviews the plans. They get advice from the Technical Advisory Board, which is composed of chief researchers from shareholder companies. The plans are then reviewed by the board of directors, which also consists of one representative from each of the shareholders. So the overall research agenda is set almost completely by the industry participants.

Should the research agenda be subject to wider review? John Pinkston thinks not. "I don't feel the need for any additional information or advice," he says. The board of directors is composed exclusively of shareholder members. Although the bylaws would permit two outside directors, none has been appointed to date. Neither the University of Texas or the academic community at large holds any formal advisory position at MCC.

Just as the MCC falls midway between an industrial and university laboratory, its research agenda falls approximately on the midpoint between a specialist's selective approach and a generalist's integrated program. Most of the research is software based. There is, for example, no wafer fabrication laboratory as at the MCNC or the CIS—a significant weakness according to some outside observers since it cuts the researcher out of having day-to-day contact with the hardware production environment. "When I get calls from TV people," remarks Stotesbery, "it's tough, because there's nothing to see. No robots, no exotic machinery, just groups of offices with simple terminals clustered around a computer room."

There is of course some hardware activity including a recently added semiconductor packaging lab. This allows a program to focus on the physical pins and packaging of computer chips. And semiconductor wafers can be fabricated in shareholder's plants. But there is no work, as yet, on advanced hardware materials, such as gallium arsenide chips, which many think are critical to a successful Fifth Generation project.

Does the project suffer because it doesn't cover the hardware to software spectrum from A to Z? "We identify new program areas according to shareholder interest," says chief scientist Pinkston. "I always have to ask the question, 'is there enough common shareholder interest to justify a new project?' I think the creative process works best when you combine having enough applied research to keep the wolf from the door, and sufficient flexibility and discretion to follow up when real creativity occurs." To date, discretionary budgets are few; on the other hand, the consortium officers prefer to focus on being sure the base of applied research is well grounded "to keep the wolf from the door" and to satisfy shareholder needs.

The Elusive University Connection

During 1983, before MCC had decided to locate in Austin, there was an enormous flurry of publicity given to the race among leaders of some fifty-seven cities in the United States to lure MCC to locate in their hometown. Collected newspaper clippings as fat as Webster's dictionary attest to the campaign to attract this allegedly lucrative high-tech investment. Even after Austin was chosen from four finalists (the others were Atlanta, San Diego, and Research Triangle in North Carolina), the ripple effect continued. Atlanta developed its own center, the California legislature appropriated more money for other centers. A major reason, at least in Inman's mind, why Austin was chosen was the commitments undertaken by the University of Texas at Austin and by Texas A&M to build their electrical engineering and computer science programs.

The build up was done in archtypical Texas fashion. Through a task force assembled by Democratic Governor Mark White, who had started to diversify the Texas economy of oil and cattle, the University agreed to a lavish list of "offerings," which ultimately lured the MCC. This clearly put the University into the front seat as a pivotal catalyst for development in the Austin region. It testifies to the enormous economic leverage that can be exercised by an academic institution that understands the importance of the technology mission. The list included:

- Establishing a $15 million endowment to support the full range of faculty positions in the electrical engineering and computer science departments. Five million dollars of this would support at least six chairs with senior scholars.
- Creating thirty new faculty positions in microelectronics and computer science over three years.
- Establishing graduate fellowships with $750,000 per year. These have indeed started, and master's or doctoral students receive some $1,000 per month, tax free, over two years.
- Increasing research support in microelectronics and computer science by $1 million per year.
- Providing $5 million worth of new equipment.
- And leasing land located at Balcones Research Campus to MCC for ten years at $1 per year.

The first thing that happened, after these terms had been offered and MCC moved to Austin, was also archtypically Texan. An anonymous donor gave $8 million to the University, a sum that was matched, and matched again, creating a hefty $32 million that will result in 32 new chairs. Sixteen of these are to be in engineering, 12 of them at $1 million each, and 4 at $1.4 million.

But the story doesn't stop here. Again, Texas is like no other state, and its university system is like no other in the country. In most universities, the interest from the endowments would pay the chairholders salary. Not so in Austin. Since the University is public, the legislature pays the salaries. The interest from endowments is used as salary supplements and also to cover research expenditures, administrative support, and other costs that would make professors from any other setting turn green with envy. Texas professors, instead, are green with money.

But despite all this highly leveraged activity, the connections between the University of Texas and the MCC are still at the "informal" stage—which is where they were designed to be. Ben Streetman is the director of UT's new microelectronics research center. Originally a graduate of UT, he had spent seventeen years on the faculty of the University of Illinois. In 1982, they lured him back to Texas with the offer of an endowed chair. Just before coming home, he had been a consultant with the group in North Carolina that set up MCNC. He and Professor John Linvill from Stanford had assisted Bill Friday in the design of MCNC. Back in Austin, Streetman got a call one day from Governor White's office. They wanted him to come discuss how MCC could be attracted to Austin. "I knew it was serious when I walked in the room and saw all the brass," he said. Streetman is credited as playing an important role in attracting MCC to Austin.

What makes all of this so intriguing is that Streetman and the microelectronic research center have little or nothing to do with MCC's research program. "Our work is focusing on the next generation of materials, like gallium arsenide. We'd like to build a vacuum crystal-growing facility. I expect we'll apply for funding to the SRC or perhaps to NSF for funds to develop our work and also build an industrial affiliates program." Nonetheless, the aura of MCC has had a dramatic effect. "We can shoot for the Nobel Laureates now. Not just because MCC is here, but because we now have enough funding to invite three or four superstars instead of one. Superstars cluster together. They don't want to come to Texas and stick out like a sore thumb."

There are, of course, many informal links between MCC and UT, as well as between MCC and Texas A&M, although again an unexpected beneficial by-product was the establishment of good relations between UT and Texas A&M. "First time we'd talked to those guys in a long time," said one UT senior administrator. Many MCC researchers hold adjunct professorships at one or both of the schools. John Pinkston, MCC's chief scientist, holds two such positions and teaches or participates in symposia at both campuses.

Some of the MCC staff come from the University of Texas—one of the officers who heads the artificial intelligence program, Woodman Bledsoe, is on leave of absence from UT. But as Inman notes, MCC had an explicit policy *against* recruiting at UT, because it could easily be misconstrued as raiding the campus. Further down the ranks there are a few other MCC direct hires whose last employment was UT. Nevertheless, there are more former IBMers and ex-Bell Lab people than former UT faculty. Inman also notes that, to date, MCC has hired very few newly graduated students. In fact, the average experience level of MCC's Ph.D.'s is fourteen years. Again, this link of hiring the output of UT's electrical engineering and computer science programs will take place, informally, and with time.

MCC is planning to create "university affiliates program." Schools like MIT, CMU, Minnesota, Florida State, and others outside Texas—as well as the University of Houston, UT, and Texas A&M within the state—will be invited to join. The purpose will be to share nonproprietary research results with the academic community. This is not likely to be a source of research funding, although it is conceivable that in the future MCC could turn to universities to subcontract some of its work.

In a similar vein, MCC has launched an industrial associates program. There are already thirteen members—among them Tracor, Quotron, Celanese, Norton, Magnavox, SAI, and GTE. Depending on sales volume, each associate pays a flat $25,000 to $150,000 to participate in symposia where nonproprietary research results are disclosed. Periodic newsletters and reports are received as well. The main idea is that these are smaller companies who are also suppliers to the industry. Thus, the reasoning goes, they need to get prepared to supply new products and services.

Technology Transfer

"The weakest link in the chain," says Inman, "is the technology transfer issue. We've seen how to make the most effective use of educated talent—those educated to create technology—even where in the country as a whole we have a decreasing pool of such talent. But the real premium now is on speed—the speed of transferring technology from lab to production line." How will they do it?

Palle Smidt, senior vice president for plans and programs, has technology transfer as one of his major responsibilities. On a day-to-day basis, he will be looking at how to get new ideas into industrial production in the shareholder companies. One way this is done is through "liaison" personnel. For each program they fund, every shareholder assigns one person to MCC who spends 75 percent of his or her time working on MCC research and the balance on communication between MCC and the shareholder. The liaison person is seen as "the company point man" at MCC with a responsibility of identifying or developing a "receptor" organization within his or her own company. A one-person limit per program is upped to two people for the larger Advanced Computer Architecture program.

Quality and commitment is a potential problem here. Admiral Inman, who has been able to insist on the highest caliber people for all his hires, has the least influence in this category. This job requires special talent, someone who can both work at the cutting edge of science and technology and translate new knowledge into terms management and operations people can understand. MCC will surely be a catalyst in accelerating the rate of technology transfer. But only recently has it started to define explicit management policies and techniques to achieve it. Its success will depend to a large degree on the effectiveness of the "point men and women" in making the transfer—exactly those people over whom Inman has least control.

Changing the Odds

"This [MCC] is a whole new way of doing business," exclaims George Black, human resources vice president, formerly from RCA. "This pooling of intellectual and financial resources is an idea whose time has come."

Is it? And if so, to what extent? Cooperative research is indeed something relatively new for the electronics industry. Perhaps more than most industries, electronics has compressed the race from start-up to maturity into a shorter timespan than has automobiles or textiles. As an industry matures, as parts of the computer and electronics industry are beginning to do (for example, standard business data processing on large mainframe computers), the form of innovation changes. In a maturing industry, entrepreneurial innovation is superceded by cooperative change. Partly this is due to the laws of diminishing returns. R&D becomes more expensive, the next quantum leaps become more complex.

While it is true that each early generation of computers proceeded more and more quickly, this may not be so with the Fifth Generation. The reason is that in this area we have hit a temporary plateau. A number of major breakthroughs will be necessary to create machines with speech and vision capabilities. Many of the top MCC people welcome the chance to work on something of national and strategic importance.

It was this national and strategic importance that first motivated Bill Norris of CDC, now retired. "More than any other," says Inman, "Norris was the key strategist. People like me, I'm just the implementor, the one who executes the strategy."

Now that MCC is in full swing, Norris, its original strategist, has stepped to the sidelines. Surprisingly, he has never visited MCC at the Austin site, nor is he a member of the MCC board of directors. Once he saw the strategy was working, he left it to others to carry on—"Texas style."

Part V
CONCLUSION

Chapter 12

WHAT IF. . .

We have found what amounts to a paradigm of successful behavior in our own high-tech industrial sector. . . . The universities led the way in basic research and development; entrepreneurs provided the energy and skills needed to develop products and get them to market; and the government provided funds—often first to the universities in the form of development grants and research support, and later to the emerging new enterprises as an eager customer.

The question we now face is whether this formula can be extended successfully, or whether it must be modified before it can be applied to other economic sectors.

Joseph Duffey, Chancellor
University of Massachusetts at Amherst
February 1986 [New England's Role in Enhancing America's Competitiveness, Highlights of a Conference, October 24-25, 1985, Amherst, Mass.]

The Reagan Administration plans to cut federally financed research at colleges and universities by hundreds of millions of dollars in the next few years as part of its effort to trim the budget deficit.

New York Times, March 20, 1986

"What if . . . ," said Professor Linvill. "Ask that question in the conclusion of your study." What if these consortia do succeed? What if their numbers continue to proliferate?

What are the prospects? Marc Tucker views the advent of research and development consortia with a cool dose of practicality. "If you were to look at these consortia as the principal instrument for adjusting to the problems that we face economically, I would have to say: 'Ridiculous.' They don't begin to get at the larger problems that we face. On their own terms, though, they are incredibly valuable contributions." His observation opens the question as to whether the scale of the response represented by industry-university consortia is commensurate with the sense of threat and survival felt by American industry.

"One Hundred Consortia Bloom . . ."

An appropriate response would have to alter the behavior of our institutions—education, government, and business—to reflect the technological transition our economy and working life have experienced. In this sense, consortia, although still few in number, portend a potentially significant trend. They signal a fundamental realignment of our institutions. Universities, particularly the leading 100 research institutions, in partnership with industry and government are moving to fulfill a technology agenda directly affecting regional or national economic development. This is happening to a far greater degree and with greater sense of urgency than at any time since World War II. The reason is simply that an unprecedented post-war period of wealth creation—when the United States was essentially the only show in town—was followed by a steady erosion in productivity starting late in the 1960s.

The first answer, then, to the what if question is that more consortia, properly capitalized and led, could well serve to accelerate the move toward a national technology agenda. This raises immediate questions of national policy. Should the federal government—following the recent lead of numerous state governments—not put substantial resources to work to fuel this trend? If the evidence put forth in this book offers a tentative answer and if the NSF Engineering Research Centers program, although modestly funded, provides a federal mechanism to build on, then the answer should be yes. Whatever administration follows the Reagan era, the national challenge will be to restore competitive vitality to the U.S. economy in world markets. Consortia building will be a significant building block in meeting the challenge.

A shift in national priorities, in contrast to the basic research federal agenda of the post-World War II decades, should stress the importance of collaborative technology initiatives. A nationally inspired effort to think out a technology strategy—conceptualized by the president's science advisor and Office of Science and Technology—might stimulate the creation of many more R&D consortia. What would be the right number or technical focus? One Hundred may be a target number in complementary fields. What would be the right amount of money? Two to 3 percent of a bloated defense budget, or about $5 to $10 billion, redirected to economic ends, might do the job. That means about an investment of $100 million to $50 million per year per consortium. These collaborative efforts, as suggested in the opening pages of this book would serve to eliminate an immense amount of duplicated and costly research in selected industrial fields. Manufacturing science, as described by James Koontz, is one example.

"One Hundred Departmental Barriers Wither . . ."

A corollary to what if there were more consortia, is what if they were focused on integrated or interdisciplinary problem-solving teamwork. If a majority of today's and tomorrow's consortia are university based, can we not expect them to serve as more than what was described earlier in this book as ''impedence managers?'' If the problems of our times, many of them technologically complex, call for integrating disciplines in resolving them, should our academic institutions not follow suit by diminishing the relevance of intellectually entrenched departmental disciplines. A student or practitioner narrowly versed in finance or electrical engineering or Shakespearean literature must become equally adept at integrating knowledge between seemingly disparate fields.

Such a proposition should not be equated with an advocacy of no disciplines. Rather, it is the power of any one department to limit intellectual boundaries through narrow degree requirements or shortsighted penalties for faculty crossing into new fields—not to speak of working on industry problems—that is challenged. Indeed, if history serves us, it is in reminding the academic community of the radical changes instituted by making the "mechanical and agricultural arts" respectable fields with the birth of the land grant college system more than a hundred years ago. As we near the twenty-first century, the time has come for similar radicalism in reconstructing the "departmental intellect" of universities. In this regard, consortia are providing a vital, if not unexpected, impetus for academic constraints to be overcome through interdisciplinary or integrated research.

"One Hundred Management Experiments Are Sown . . ."

Transfer of technology was discussed repeatedly throughout this book. While this subject leads in variety of directions, the most critical may be that somewhere along the way U.S. managers haven't kept pace. The imperative of change implicit in technology transfer in a global economy has been overshadowed by financial criteria in measuring corporate success. It isn't so much that we've lost the magic of creating new ideas or new technologies. We still do that very well. Rather, it is that ideas no longer flow into the marketplace as rapidly or effectively as in the past. What's worse is that others are doing it better. A big part of American enterprise, despite flurries of best-selling management books and myriad change consultants, still coasts on pervasive organizational philosophies matured over more than eighty years out of Tayloristic "scientific management." Part of the price of this evolution is that it has built structures, habits, and reflexes that inhibit the flow of information. What results is that new knowledge is overlooked or is not transferred to maximum economic benefit.

What if 100 consortia, whether initiated by industry, academe, or government, induced a hundred experiments in finding a new system of management appropriate to a knowledge-driven economic age. For this to happen effectively, the relationship between new technologies and new management philosophies will have to become a centerpiece of current or future consortia. It is not enough, otherwise, to superimpose new technologies on outdated management structures. If America is involved in toughened global competition that pits management skills against one another, a quantum leap must be made in inventing better concepts of organization. That leap has yet to be made. Knowledge is going to have to be treated as a strategic ingredient with information as its raw material; financial experts are going to have to learn the particularities of laboratory scientists; engineers are going to have to talk to nonengineers; technologists are going to have to mediate relationships between makers and users of knowledge-intensive tools; and business schools are going to have to stop producing MBAs only superficially prepared to cope with new technologies and their strategic implications.

One is reminded of the importance of letting one hundred management experiments take seed by the enlightened insights of former Governor James Hunt of North Carolina in a passage he wrote in *Global Stakes* in 1982. "We have not mastered the process of innovation," he stated then. "Technological innovation consists of two interrelated parts: technical and organizational innovation. . . . Organizational innovation can occur on a large scale, such as at the national level—or it can be on a small scale, such as in an office or industrial firm." To illustrate his point he quoted Professor Don Price of Harvard University in reference to studies the latter had completed on the World War II period. "The most significant discovery or development for science and technology to come from the war effort," said Price, "was not the technical secrets that were involved in radar or the atomic bomb. It was the administrative system and set of operating policies that produced such technological feats." They worked in fueling our economy tc world dominance. Governor Hunt's admonitions and Professor Price's findings are a fitting backdrop to what the consortia phenomenon may represent.

What if consortia are the experiment that leads to a new system of administering our economic future? They may indeed become, as Professor John Linvill states, "important beyond our highest expectations."

Appendixes

Appendix A
Consortia Fact Sheets

PROJECT ATHENA (ATHENA)

Location   Massachusetts Institute of Technology
                     Cambridge, Massachusetts

Focus   A five-year experiment aimed at campus-wide
                     integration of interactive graphics and computers

Founded

May 83   Project Athena announced
September 1983   75 PCs, work stations, and terminals delivered
January 1986   600 PCs, workstations, and terminals delivered

Funding

MIT $20 million (paid over five years)
                         $10–11 million faculty curriculum
                         $ 9–10 million operating cost
Companies $50 million (equipment)
DEC   fifty three VAX 11/750s and 11/780s, 300 termi-
                     nals, and DEC staff support
IBM   500 work stations, 145 IBM XTs, 160 IBM ATs,
                     and staff support

Partners

University (1)   Massachusetts Institute of Technology
Companies (3)   Digital Equipment Corporation
                     IBM Corporation
                     Codex Corporation (donated hardware design of
                     network)
Plus   Bolt Beranek & Newman has a part-time staff
                     person on loan

As of early 1986   Steve Lerman, project director
                     Maurice Wilkes of DEC and Charles Salisbury of
                     IBM are primary company contacts

                     Project working groups include:
                     graphics, real-time data acquisition, database soft-
                     ware, documentation, electronic classroom, man-
                     agement software, statistics and econometrics,
                     numerical analysis, interactive video

140

ATHENA (continued)

Total Users: 5000 (eligible students)
Equipment: 43 VAXs, 300 terminals, 50 VAX stations, 160 IBM PC/ATs, and 140 IBM PC/XTs

Project Athena at MIT could be considered a "reverse consortium" as are several others like the Carnegie-Mellon relationship that was announced in 1981 with IBM. In these cases, the major focus is on a university application rather than on an industrial one. While technology transfer is a two-way street, in this case the transfer is first to the university campus and secondly to the industrial partners. We can learn a lot about other consortia that seek to solve industry problems by looking closely at "reverse" cases like Athena.

The Athena project has a clear vision, initiated by several MIT faculty members. The goal is to develop a new coherent computing environment for students and faculty across the entire campus. A new work station is envisaged and a network established to link large numbers of users.

POSITIVES: The project has engaged the energies not just of the direct project staff but of many faculty and students in a wide variety of fields—not only engineering but also foreign languages and writing. The wide participation level is reflected in the many committees, including a Student Information Processing Committee. The issue of who owns patents and licenses has been solved—MIT owns them. There have been notable technical successes, such as a new window system, successful implementation of UNIX, and sheer size: there are now 5,000 students eligible to use the system.

ISSUES: One issue is money. While the overall five-year budget of $70 million sounds large, the amount available to an individual faculty member for project development is surprisingly small—on the order of $20,000 per year.

Another issue is a slippage in the schedule. One reason for this is that initial expectations of a "new order of magnitude of computing" and 3000 work stations of a new type may have been too optimistic. Interestingly, the same "slow delivery" issue surfaced at Carnegie-Mellon University in its agreement with IBM. One hypothesis is that the problem stems from market forces: The IBM PC was commercially so successful that the company is reluctant to develop and introduce a new competing work station. MIT has had past experiments like Athena—Multics and IBM timesharing (CTSS) for example. Neither of these experiments were adopted as industry standards, yet much new knowledge was gained for both company sponsors and the university.

CENTER FOR ADVANCED OPTICAL TECHNOLOGY (CAOT)
(A New York State Center for Advanced Technology)

Location	Institute of Optics, University of Rochester Rochester, New York
Focus	Basic research in the field of advanced optics
Founded	1983

Funding

State	$1 million from state/year
Companies	$1 million from companies/year

Partners

Government (1)	State of New York (NY State Science and Technology Foundation)
Academic institution (5)	Institute of Optics, University of Rochester Rochester Institute of Technology Monroe Community College
Companies (6)	Bausch and Lomb Corning Company General Electric IBM Corporation Kodak Corporation Xerox Corporation
As of early 1986	Kenneth J. Teegarden, director 300+ undergraduate majors involved 150 graduate students enrolled in program Basic research is conducted in six specialty areas; each specialty area has a named principal investigator

CAOT (continued)

The University of Rochester optics program is more then fifty years old and is the only department in the United States to offer the B.S., M.S., and Ph.D. degrees in optics. The CAOT Rochester program is considered by its staff to be a true research consortium as opposed to an applied or development consortium. Much of the work focuses on fiber optics, where everyone agrees something big is bound to happen, but no one knows exactly what it will be. Companies participate in research because they want to be sufficiently knowledgeable to take action when the market crystallizes. In contrast, a similar consortium established by the Batelle Institute has become mired in disagreements over its developmental focus and pressures to commercialize results in what is an uncertain commercial market.

The CATs program includes seven consortia

University	Research Area	Number of Corporate Sponsors
Columbia	Computers and information systems	7
Cornell	Biotechnology in agriculture	3
Polytechnic Institute	Telecommunications	7
Rochester	Advanced optical technology	6
SUNY Buffalo	Health care instruments/devices	2
SUNY Stonybrook	Medical biotechnology	11
Syracuse	Computer applications and software engineering	9

These are not the only industry-university consortia in New York State. Rensselaer Polytechnic Institute in Troy, New York, has an interlinked set of four centers, also supported by state funds.

The National Science Foundation in March 1985 announced its $200 million grant for supercomputers to be divided over five years among four universities— Cornell, Princeton, Illinois, and California (San Diego).

Cornell expects to receive an average of $8 million per year for five years from NSF. It hopes to raise another $30 million in equipment from IBM and Floating Point Systems. This would make the project about the size of Project Athena at MIT.

QUOTE from principal investigator: "Research consortia can act as catalysts for innovation. One thing I am certain of is that research in many of the high-technology areas is likely to be effective only if sustained for a long time

CAOT (continued)

at a substantial level. To me, an investment of minimum of ten years seems appropriate for any truly new technology."

The bigger picture: New York State is implementing a comprehensive strategy. The Rochester program is part of the CATs program. The strategy is led by the New York State Science and Technology Foundation. It is governed by the state commissioner of commerce, the state commissioner of education, and nine senior executives from leading high technology companies and the investment community.

QUOTE from Governor Mario Cuomo: "The creation of the Centers for Advanced Technology forges a partnership between government and two of New York's greatest strengths—its universities and its leading centers of corporate research and development. With their emphasis on R&D, education, and interaction between business and universities, these Centers . . . will serve as a focal point for the development of technologies that will shape our economy . . . into the twenty-first century."

CENTER FOR CERAMICS RESEARCH (CCR)
An Advanced Technology Center of New Jersey

Location   Rutgers University, New Brunswick, New Jersey

Focus   One of a network of advanced technology centers at public and private institutions in the areas of advanced ceramics plus three others: biotechnology, food science, and hazardous and toxic substance management

Founded   1982

  July 1982   Governors Commission on Science and Technology formed

  January 1984   Commission recommends Advanced Technology Centers and $90 million bond issue

  October 1984   Bond issue passed by New Jersey voters

Funding

  State $9 million ($1.5 million/yr for six years) for the Ceramics Research Center to be matched by $1.7 million from outside sources
Public funds out of $90 million bond issue for ATCs approved November 1984 of which: $42 million for construction of centers, $15 million for future technology centers, $23 million for undergraduate engineering improvement at New Jersey Universities, $10 million South Jersey construction for engineering computer science at community colleges

  Companies $1,120,000/yr committed at $35,000/yr per company (currently 32 company partners)

Partners

  Government (2)   State of New Jersey Governor's Commission on Science and Technology
National Science Foundation

  Academic Research   Rutgers University
  Institutions (1)

CCR (continued)

Companies (32)

Alcoa
Allied Signal Inc.
AT&T Technologies Inc.
Borg Warner Corp.
Carpenter Tech. Corp.
Celanese Research Co.
Corning Glass Works
Dow Corning
Dow Chemical USA
Dresser Industries
E.I. DuPont deMemoures and Co.
Englehard Corp.
Ferro Corp.
FMC Corp.
Frenchtown Ceramics Co.
W.R. Grace & Co.
GTE Laboratories
Hexcel Corp.
IBM
Johnson & Johnson Dental Products Co.
Lockheed Electronics
Martin Marietta Labs
National Bureau of Standards
Norton Company
RCA Corp.
Rhone-Poulenc Inc.
Rolls-Royce Inc.
Sohio Engineered Materials Comp.
Solvay Technologies Corp.
3M Co.
Union Carbide

As of early 1986

Edward Barr, chairman of the Governor's Commission
Edward Cohen, program director
Malcolm McLaren, chairman, Department of Ceramics
John Wachtman, director of Center for Ceramics Research

CCR (continued)

Future Plans

The Governor's Commission is currently implementing four technology centers, and new areas of advanced technology are being considered in light of overwhelming public support for the bond issue

Other Advanced Technology Centers

Biotechnology: New Jersey Institute of Technology (NJIT), Rutgers University, and the University of Medicine and Dentistry of New Jersey
Hazardous and Toxic Substance Management: NJIT, Stevens Institute of Technology, University of Medicine and Dentistry, and Rutgers University
Food Technology: Cook College of Rutgers University

A pertinent synopsis of the CCR was provided in a *New York Times* article entitled: "Should Rutgers Ring the Bell?

"Rutgers Presses Efforts to Join Top Tier of Universities in U.S." It cites industry-university consortia as a key point in Rutgers' bid for excellence for which the New Jersey government issued a high-tech bond for financial support.

. . . When it was clear that the bond issue had passed overwhelmingly, Rutgers administrators signalled their victory by ringing the rarely used 160-year-old bells on top of Old Queens, the historic campus building where they work.

Some faculty members are still dubious. 'Just because something is high tech doesn't mean it is good tech,' said Terry A. Matilsky, an associate professor of physics, arguing that corporate research needs will inevitably impinge on the freedom of academic researchers.

'Not so,' said Malcolm G. McLaren, the chairman of the ceramics department and a key figure in the creation of a center that is investigating the potential use of ceramics in computers. . . . He contends that such centers ought to be part of the mission of a public university, just as agricultural research was for most of the institution's early life. 'The post Industrial era runs on Ph.D.'s and there is a need for new forms of partnership that didn't exist ten years ago.'

The question this article raises is whether Rutgers administrators were justified by the event to ring the 160-year-old bell.

QUOTE: "New Jersey is in a position of national leadership in critical areas like education, environmental protection, and job creation." (Governor Thomas H. Kean, Annual Message to the New Jersey State Legislature, January 8, 1985)

147

COMPUTER INTEGRATED DESIGN, MANUFACTURING, AND AUTOMATION CENTER (CIDMAC)

Location	Purdue University West Lafayette, Indiana
Focus	Automated Manufacturing Technologies
Founded	January 1982
Funding	
Capital	$5 million—$200,000/yr per sponsor company plus equipment value of $25,000/yr per affiliate company
University	Construction money and services
Operating	$1.1–2.5 million/yr
Partners	
University (1) Companies (6)	Purdue University Alcoa Cincinnati Milacron Control Data Corp. Cummins Engine Co. Ransburg Corp. TRW, Inc.
As of January 1986	Director: Henry T. Yang, dean of engineering 5 industry representatives 31 faculty associated 32 student teams involving 47 students

NOTE: In 1985, CIDMAC was complemented by the creation of the larger Engineering Research Center (ERC) for Intelligent Manufacturing Systems, funded by a five-year, $17 million NSF grant. By summer 1986, ERC will consist of 40 faculty, 120 graduate students, and 80 undergraduates.

CIDMAC (continued)

CIDMAC demonstrates the successful single-handed initiative of a visionary *engineering dean*. This is a case of a university that was willing to invest and risk its own cash resources to ensure the success of the venture. CIDMAC's goal is to address the full spectrum of technology issues relating to automated manufacturing, e.g., a full interdisciplinary approach. "We're doing generic research," says a company sponsor. An unexpected outcome of the center's modern, glassed-in manufacturing laboratory on the campus is to put engineering into the forefront as a coveted field for the best students on campus.

POSITIVES: Several characteristics of CIDMAC stand out as unique and important. (1) Early in the process of planning the Center's mission, industry and university labored together for almost a year to evolve complementary "wish lists." From this emerged common working ground and trust between the company sponsors and the campus-based researchers. (2) The research is long term and open ended. Industry sponsors have made five-year commitments. Company sponsors are careful not to impose "commercial" deadlines on research. (3) The architecture and setting of the center's facilities are not insignificant factors in creating a positive image for the center in the minds of students. (4) The Center's activities have brought a "real life" tone to campus research. This has caused soul searching by other academic whose own research agendas might be labeled "out-of-sync" with real-life applications.

ISSUES: The primary negative, as industry sees it, may lie in the open-ended, long-term research commitment by industry sponsors. It is not clear how long the sponsoring divisional managers can sustain a large infusion of research dollars without feeling increasing "front-office" pressures to produce measurable results.

QUOTE from Jerry Schlensker, vice president for manufacturing at Cummins Engine: "If I had to do projects internally for $200K a year, that would get me 2 or 3 people only. At Purdue, you get 50 to 75 people and a door to bounce ideas through. In addition, you can share knowledge with other participants. That's cost effective."

QUOTE from Larry Hollingshead, manager, Artificial Intelligence Group at Cincinnati Milacron: "We're much more involved now because we're beginning to see benefits. One of them is the people we've hired from CIDMAC. They're just excellent. Their exposure to manufacturing through CIDMAC meant they were productive to us almost at once. They had tools and capabilities. Our sustained commitment to CIDMAC is due to the foresight of our R&D VP. Support was always there from the top down."

CENTER FOR INDUSTRIAL INNOVATION (CII)
Including:
Center for Interactive Computer Graphics (CIG)
Center for Manufacturing Productivity (CMP)
Integrated Electronics Center (IEC)

Location	Rensselaer Polytechnical Institute Troy, New York
Focus	Industrial-oriented advanced technology research and development (indirectly linked to a 1200-acre Technology/Industrial Park and a Business Incubator Program)
Founded	CII—1984 CIG—1977 —1979 (industrial associates program) CMP—1979 IEC—1980

Funding

CII
$30 million for building (New York State)
$30 million committed by RPI in equipment to CII ($24 million is in place, $6 million to be used for refurbishing)
$ 6 million in combined corporate research funding (the three subcenters (CIG, CMP, CIE) each average $2 million/yr in research)

CIG
$1 million in seed money from NSF
Now totally industry funded ($1.9 million/yr, 38 cos @ $50,000/yr)

CMP
10 cos lifetime membership @ $300,000
8 cos sustaining membership @ $120,000 for 3 yrs
15 cos non-members with research commitments
CIM (Computer Integrated Manufacturing): 7 cos funding a 3-yr contract at $7 million
AFT (Automated Fastening Technology): 5 cos funding a 3-yr contract at $650,000
FMS (Flexible Manufacturing Systems): 5 cos funding a 3-yr contract at $650,000

150

CII (continued)

	AIM (Artificial Intelligence for Manufacturing): 2 cos funding a 3-yr contract at $650,000; 4-6 more cos added in 1986
	APP (Advanced Powder Processing): seeking 20 cos sponsors for 3-yr contract at $25 per year (small company focus)
IEC	$13 million in facilities
	$ 2 million/yr in research (25 cos)

Partners

Government (1)	State of New York
University (1)	Rensselaer Polytechnic Institute
Companies	CII: 90 companies
	Including:
	CIG: 38 companies
	CMP: 18 companies
	CIM: 7 cos
	AFT: 5 cos
	FMS: 5 cos
	AIM: 2 cos (4-6 more in 1986)
	APP: seeking 20 cos for 1987
	IEC: 25 cos
	Tech Park: 28 cos (600 employees)
	Incubator: 18 cos

As of January 1986

Chris LeMaistre, director, CII
Dr. Michael J. Wozny, director, CIG
Dr. Leo Hanifin, director, CMP
Dr. Andrew Steckel, director CIE
Jerry Mahone, director, Incubator Program
Mike Wacholder, director, Industrial Park

CII (continued)

RPI's Center for Industrial Innovation (CII) is one of the largest and most extensive university-based programs. CII is an umbrella group to coordinate the activities of what had until 1982 been three separate centers—the Interactive Computer Graphics Center, the Integrated Electronics Center, and the Center of Manufacturing Productivity and Technology. The latter, the CMP, also has a special Computer Integrated Manufacturing program, considered by many to be among the best in the country. Likewise, the Interactive Graphics Center has state of the art equipment and is considered one of the leaders in this field.

POSITIVES: The formation of CII is the centerpiece of a strategy to move RPI from an undergraduate teaching program to a graduate, research-based technology university. The RPI 2000 Plan foresees making RPI a peer to CMU and CalTech. The centerpiece of CII is a new "integrated building" that has been strategically located at the gateway to the campus in order to "change the culture of the established university." "Integrated building" refers to intermixing the offices of the three different centers in order to increase synergy among them. The building and the Center have attracted a lot of attention and funds, and could make a major contribution toward revival of the Troy economy into becoming, in the hopeful words of CII's director, the "Silicon Valley of the Hudson."

NEGATIVES: Despite the proximity of GE (Schenectady), there is little infrastructure outside CII to draw upon. For example, the first successful incubator company (Raster Technologies) had to move out of Troy and locate near Boston in order to find qualified employees. Another problem is the difficulty in shifting from a teaching to a research environment. The academic structure does not presently reward industry researchers, who have no clear path toward tenure.

QUOTE: "This [the teaching/research split] is the single greatest issue that we're trying to break down." Mary Johnson, manager of Corporate Relations, Interactive Computer Graphics Center.

QUOTE: "No one will be able to ignore the statement our new building makes. The RPI goal is to produce a 'steeple of excellence.' " Chris LeMaistre, CII director.

CENTER FOR INTEGRATED SYSTEMS (CIS)

Location Stanford University
Palo Alto, California

Focus Integrated semiconductor design and fabrication, particularly for computer and information systems

Founded January 1980
Building inaugurated in January 1985

Funding

Companies $15 million (for building):
@ $750,000/co for building fund
$ 5.9 million (for equipment):
64 co donors of equipment
University land and services
Federal gov't $8 million 3-year research grant
Related gov't support $40 million total affiliated faculty research budget
$21 million for integrated circuits, solid state, computer science, and computer systems areas
Operating support $2.4 million CIS sponsor cos
(@$120,000/yr per co)
$2.5 million from the SRC
$5 million from other industry

Partners

University (1) Stanford University

Companies (20)

DEC	Fairchild
General Electric	Gould/AMI
GTE	Hewlett-Packard
Honeywell/Synertek	IBM
Intel	ITT
Monsanto	Motorola
Northrop	Philips/Signetics
Rockwell International	Tektronix
Texas Instruments	TRW
United Technologies	Xerox

(plus 64 equipment donors)

CIS (continued)

As of January 1986   John Linvill and James Meindl, co-directors
                                      79 faculty and 83 affiliated faculty
                                      6 industrial visitors

The CIS is an exemplary illustration of *industry-university leadership in funding of a consortium*. By intent, government money was kept out at the "front-end" in order to minimize program constraints. Though corporate dollars built the CIS' facilities and equipped them, corporate members have been assiduous in not playing an intrusive role in setting the research agenda. The strategy, successfully executed to date, was to rely on government research grants (federal) as a major source of ongoing operating funds.

POSITIVES: While its sleek building and labs are similar to the cousin MCNC in North Carolina, the CIS is linked to a single university rather than several. Among its achievements to date: (1) breaking down departmental barriers by bringing various disciplines to bear on its research agenda, (2) successful efforts to bridge an industry labeled "cultural gap" between hardware and software people, and (3) the transfer of knowledge has worked informally, efficiently, and with enthusiasm by virtue of the frequent campus to industry and industry to campus visits.

ISSUES: A residue of departmental turf protection remains. Electrical engineering has a more privileged position on campus in contrast to computer science which belongs under the humanities. This has led to growing pains. For example, when French President Miterrand visited the CIS in 1984, someone forgot to invite the computer science faculty. Strong efforts have being made to overcome such difficulties.

QUOTE from George Pake, vice president for research, Xerox Corporation (CIS co-founder): "I insisted from the very beginning on industry maintaining an arm's-length relationship with faculty."

QUOTE from Professor John Linvill, CIS co-director: "The time has really come for the industrial sector to couple with universities. There's no free lunch. There are enormous opportunities that benefit all sectors."

CORPORATION FOR SCIENCE AND TECHNOLOGY (CST)

Location	Indianapolis, Indiana
Focus	High-technology research and development grants, technological advice, and financial and business counseling
Founded	1982
Funding	$10 million annual state appropriation
Partners	CST Board Members

Chairman	Chairman, Methodist Health Foundation
Three politicians	Lieutenant Governor, Indiana
	One Member, Indiana House of Reps.
	One Member, Indiana State Senate
Nine academic institutions	President, Ball State
	President, Indiana State University
	President, Indiana University
	President, Indiana Vocational and Technical College
	President, Purdue University
	President, Rose-Hulman Institute of Technology
	President, University of Notre Dame
	President, Vincennes University
	Executive Director Support Systems, Gary Community School Corporation
Eight companies	Cook Inc., president
	Delco Electronics Corp, vice president, general manager
	Harman-Motive Inc, president
	Eli Lilly & Co, executive vice president
	G.E. Plastics Manufacturing Div, vice president and general manager
	Magnavox Government & Industrial Electronics Co., president and CEO
	Ransburg Corp, chairman and CEO
One union	UAW (Region 3), director

155

CST (continued)

Other institutions (public/nonprofit)	Corporation for Innovation Development, president
	Dept of Public Instruction (state), director
	Indiana Farm Bureau, president
	National Avionics Center
	State Board of Vocational and Technical Education, executive director
As of January 1986	John D. Hague, D.Sc., president
	54 project contacts authorized to date totaling $31,294,000
	(paid out on negotiated terms with a goal of 2 times payback to CST)

The CST is a *state-initiated* grant giving endeavor. In some ways it resembles the Benjamin Franklin program in Pennsylvania, although the latter is administered by four universities. Funding is provided by the legislature at an annual rate of $10 million. The term consortium applies, in our view, to the makeup of its board and sixteen technology-focused committees. Each represents a collective of industry, public sector, and academic representatives. While the principal activity of these committees is to determine funding priorities and to select candidates for contracts, the indirect effect is to create a broadly based network of people through whom technology transfer can flow informally. People are sitting together who otherwise would not. That indeed may be a principal constructive by-product of the CST.

POSITIVES: The CST managed in a very short period, as a result of sound leadership, to achieve the following: (1) a public awareness of the importance of new technologies to Indiana's economy, (2) a statewide network of industry-academe committees focused on specific technology issues, and (3) a grant-giving process that was kept immune from political intrusion. These grants have been constructive in stimulating individuals and small companies to step forward. Many would otherwise be cut off from grant support and/or public recognition.

ISSUES: A contractual process that is committed to making many small grants of short duration might never build a critical mass of activity sufficient to significantly affect the state's education infrastructure or the state's economy. More recently, though, sums authorized have risen to exceed $2 million per contract.

CST (continued)

Examples of early projects are taken from a CST newsletter dated November 15, 1984: "A joint research and development project by Cybotech Corporation and Purdue University is now underway following receipt of an award of $1,752,699 from the CST. The two-year project will focus on marketable robot control software packages designed to reduce or eliminate down time during the re-programming of robots." And from the same newsletter: "Custom Molded Products Incorporated of Indianopolis was awarded $90,000 to pursue federal approval of its enhanced rubber pad for tracked vehicles."

QUOTE from the CST's first president, Alden McClellan: "We do not want to be a bureaucracy. We provide seed money and we are very project oriented. Our technology committees are great in integrating university and industry interests. Informal communication is important here in building an ongoing statewide network."

INDUSTRIAL TECHNOLOGY INSTITUTE (ITI)

Location	Ann Arbor, Michigan
Focus	Advanced automated manufacturing technologies; serving small, medium and large manufacturers to upgrade productivity
Founded	1982

Funding

Capital	$17.3 million for building
	$12 million from State of Michigan
	$1.5 million challenge grant from Kresge Foundation
	$1 million from General Motors
	$.5 million from others
	$2.3 million yet to be raised
Operating	$12 million/yr in 1985

Partners

State Government	Herbert & Barbara C. Dow Foundation
Foundations (5)	W.K. Kellogg Foundation
	Kresge Foundation
	General Motors Foundation
	Charles Stewart Mott Foundation
University (1)	University of Michigan (numerous projects, joint appointments, visiting scholars)
Companies (30)	sponsors and clients (primarily industrial)
As of January 1986	Jerome Smith, president
	120 on staff
	12 faculty associates (10 universities)

ITI (continued)

The ITI is too young to evaluate on performance. Yet within a short time, it has grown in a coherent manner. It has an impressive temporary home, a large and competent staff, six company clients, and other clients coming on line. But what is significant is not so much the industry-ITI relationship, which promises to follow relatively conventional contractual arrangements for proprietary research.

Rather, what's important to us is the makeup of the ITI's founding partners: the "consortium." ITI was the creature of a governor's initiative to fund several centers of excellence. Substantial public monies were committed to create independent entities that would be of ultimate benefit to the state's economy. The next step brought a new institutional partner into the game: *foundations*. The Kellogg Foundation became an even more substantial backer than the state, committing $20 million; Dow and Mott came on with significant sums, too. The University of Michigan became an actor by offering land and access to its facilities and faculty. Industry was a follower in this case. GM came in with a $1 million pledge only after state, foundation, and university funds had legitimized and firmly grounded the ITI.

POSITIVES: The ITI has defined a clear and compelling sense of mission. Much to the credit of its director, it is proceeding without delay in implementing those goals. It has managed to develop close ties to the University of Michigan and its resources, a relationship that strengthens both partners. And it has managed to gain the backing of the state's senior companies such as GM and Ford. In this regard it has become of immediate utility to the state and national economy as a center of excellence.

ISSUES: The original intention of creating an institute that could serve the interests of out-of-date small manufacturing companies has lapsed. By committing itself to serve as a research facility working on projects of proprietary interest to clients, it is restraining the range of knowledge and technology diffusion.

MANUFACTURING ENGINEERING APPLICATIONS CENTER (MEAC)

Location	Worcester Polytechnic Institute Worcester, Massachusetts
Focus	Training program for computer-aided manufacturing (robotics primarily) and design for applications determined by member companies and MEAC
Founded	January 1981

Funding:

Companies	$50,000/yr basic membership plus contracts for services (initial donation from Emhart Corporation was in the $500,000–$750,000 range)

Partners

Academic Institution (1)	Worcester Polytechnic Institute
Companies (4)	Emhart Corp. General Electric Norton Company Digital Equipment Corp.
Former participants (contracts completed)	Cincinnati Milacron—Heald Division General Motors
As of January 1986	Donald Zwiep, chairman, MEAC Board of Directors David Asmus, director, MEAC 6 faculty members and 50 students 7 graduate students involved in specialized research

MEAC (continued)

On a spectrum from pure research to applied development, MEAC is the closest to the applications end of any of our studies. It has four industrial partners, each of whom contracts for a specific project that may be as short as 6 to 12 months. Corporate commitments are made for one year at a time. MEAC started as a joint venture between WPI and Emhart Corporation. One hundred nineteen years of industry-institute relations precede it.

POSITIVES: Where MEAC excels is technology transfer. Especially for companies just starting with new technology, MEAC delivers a finished product. We examined robotics components in use on the shop floor, delivered by MEAC. The training aspect is also very strong. Many industry people have received their reschooling at MEAC. Significant numbers of students have worked on real industry problems. We can document a number of highly successful new hires that resulted from MEAC. Another important achievement of MEAC is its effect on the structure of the institute. The mechanical engineering department has modernized, and the electrical engineering has increased in stature.

ISSUES: A major issue for MEAC is "the closer you get to product development, the harder it is to make the partnership work." While on one level MEAC works—delivering a tangible product and training students and industry personnel—on another level, industry participants have questions. The production people say they would have done better to contract with a systems house rather than a school because the job would get done faster. Higher level managers question whether new knowledge is being generated. There is clearly a debate over whether MEAC should become longer term in its focus and less applications oriented.

QUOTES: MEAC technical director: "Companies are less demanding on university researchers than their own research labs. There has been no table pounding with us! But it is very difficult to get academics to conform to industrial time tables."

A paradox : In terms of international competitiveness, one case at the General Motors Framingham plant is thought-provoking. The two MEAC senior engineers were German, part of the international exchange program with the Technical University of Berlin. After doing their work with GM, they returned to Volkswagen in Wolfsburg. Did one country gain or relinquish more or less knowledge/experience than another?

MICROELECTRONICS CENTER (MEC)

Location	Massachusetts Technology Park Corporation Westborough, Massachusetts
Focus	Semiconductor design and process engineering with a goal of supporting educational activities
Founded	1982

Funding

Capital $20 million from state (in escrow) to be matched by industry
  $6.5 million drawn (as of 1/86)
  $14 million industry equipment match

Operating $2.5 million/yr (1986)

Partners

State Government
Academic institutions (9)

Boston University
Lowell University
Massachusetts Institute of Technology
Merrimack College
Northeastern University
Southeastern Massachusetts University
Tufts University
University of Massachusetts
Worcester Polytechnic Institute

Companies (11)

Alpha Industries
Analog Devices Inc.
Data General
Digital Equipment Corp.
GCA Corp.
Phoenix Data
Polaroid
Prime Computer
Raytheon
Unitrode
U.T.I. Technologies Inc. (WANG/California)

MEC (continued)

As of January 1986   Joseph Stach, executive director
12 staff
loaned employees: 1 DEC, 1 Prime
(building program underway)

MEC came to life through the "politics" of a very political state. It illustrates what happens when politics interfere with the substance of a technology initiates—or when too many competing partners get involved too quickly. The message to anyone looking in on the MEC should be "don't do it this way." In its first three years, political egos interfered, industry leadership was fragmented, and university leadership was divided. The MEC's birth was as problematic as the MCNC's wasn't in North Carolina. One year, and possibly two, were wasted in arguments, missed signals, and petty disputes. What was lost in the process was a sense of momentum in developing a new Massachusetts groundswell in the electronics industry by strengthening the creation of semiconductor process engineers.

The MEC over a five-year period involved a broad cast of characters—most of whom knew one another but had never collaborated together before. Many were in direct competition with one another. The evolution of the MEC is partially explained by the competitive tensions between the key actors.

- Governor King vs state Senator Atkins
  Each wanted political credit for creating the MEC and rushed it into being; perhaps too fast
- Governor Dukakis vs High Tech Council
  A new governor distrusted the MEC's promoters and disagreed over its siting
- Taunton vs Westborough
  Where to put the Center: in an economically depressed town or near the electronics company sponsors
- WANG vs DEC/Data General
  Primary corporate sponsors were drawn into chosing sides by Dukakis over where to site the center; they took opposite positions and split a heretofore unified Mass High Tech Council
- Boston University vs six other universities
  BU wanted center stage, so did some others
- Governor Dukakis vs his Secretary of Economic Affairs Murphy
  They were potential political competitors; the first antagonized high-techers, the second wooed them

163

MEC (continued)

POSITIVE: The MEC is intended as an educational resource for the state's engineering schools by dispersing equipment and offering centralized wafer fabrication facilities.

ISSUES: Politicians played ball with the center. Legislation was drafted and passed before consensus was fully achieved. Governor King and his economic affairs secretary wanted to create the MEC before running a reelection effort they couldn't win. The state legislator who lobbied the MEC into being may have had his own eye more on Congress than on laying substantial groundwork for a long-term strategy. And Governor Dukakis, who inherited the MEC legislation, came into office suspicious of the high-tech business community, which in turn wasn't unified on what the function of the MEC should be. At the same time, universities had competing interests. The result was the loss of valuable time and momentum.

The MEC is one of two state technology centers with legislated $20 million matching funds authorizations in Massachusetts. Both the MEC and a new materials characterization center (its mission still under study) are administered by the Mass Tech Park Corp. Alongside them, the state, in 1985, created four new centers of excellence administered by an independent corporation through the office of the secretary of economic affairs. Only token funds were provided to implement the program. The absence of a coherent state technology strategy, in contrast to North Carolina, New York or New Jersey, is a flaw in the Massachusetts program.

MICROELECTRONICS AND COMPUTER TECHNOLOGY CORPORATION (MCC)

Location	Austin, Texas A 20-acre site within the Balcones Research Campus of the University of Texas
Focus	For-profit research with informal affiliation to Texas universities
Founded	January 1983 Research began January 1984
Funding	$50–100 million/yr (FY 1986—$65 million)
Companies	Opening price per share of stock: $150,000 Current price per share: $1,000,000
University of Texas	$15 million to support endowed faculty positions $1 million increase in research support for microelectronics and computer science $5 million in new equipment $750,000 yearly for graduate fellowships

Partners (as of 1/86)

Companies (22)

Advanced Micro Devices
Allied Corporation
Bellcore—Bell Communications Research Corporation
BMC Industries
Boeing Aircraft Corporation
Control Data Corporation
Digital Equipment Corporation
Eastman Kodak Company
Gould Inc.
Harris Corporation
Honeywell Corporation
Lockheed
Martin Marietta Corporation
Mostek Corporation
Motorola Corporation
National Semiconductor Corporation

MCC (continued)

NCR Corporation
RCA Corporation
Rockwell International Corporation
Sperry Corporation
3M Company

Industrial Associates
Program

Current members: Alcoa, Celanese, Execucom, Magnavox, Norton, Quotron, Rodgers, SAIC, Shaldahl, Sprague, Symbolics, Tracor, Zycad. Sliding scale fee of $25,000 to $150,000 to participate in symposia on non-proprietary research.

Academic ties (not
officially part of
MCC)

University of Texas and Texas A&M University University Affiliates Program: 17
They agreed to establish a communications channel with MCC for a future research dialog.

As of January 1986

Admiral Bobby Inman is COB/CEO/president
Dr. John Pinkston is the chief scientist
The board of directors is composed exclusively of shareholder members and Admiral Inman.

Jan. 84
Mar. 85

20 people on the payroll
286 people on the payroll
200 people directly engaged in technical research: 43% have Ph.D.'s, 28% have master's degrees, 75–80% come from industry of whom 45% are "assigned" or "liaison" personnel, i.e., salary continues to be paid by the home company rather than by MCC; average years of experience: 15.

Jan. 86

405 total staff
295 are scientific staff

MCC (continued)

MCC is a private, profit-making research consortium. Since it has no formal ties with the University of Texas, it does not strictly fit the definition of industry-university partnerships we use in our study. It acts like one, however, and its similarities and differences to the other consortia are instructive. The research agenda is set by the MCC director and staff with industry shareholders. Its four major research areas have time horizons of 6, 7, 8, and 10 years. Over a three-year minimum participation period, each company will invest from $10 to 15 million at the high end to $2 million at the low end.

MCC was founded in response to the Japanese challenge. It can also be viewed as a grouping of mid-sized companies responding to the IBM challenge (IBM is not an MCC shareholder). MCC falls partway between a university research lab and an industrial lab. The shareholder companies set the research agenda, though the agenda was quite well framed from the outset.

POSITIVE: A large research staff has been built in a surprisingly short time. Antitrust issues have been resolved, which sets a precedent for other consortia. It is still too early to tell whether MCC will produce a major breakthrough in computing technology, but the potential for a large payoff is certainly there. The premise is that a $2 to 10 million investment per company can leverage $50 to 100 million worth of research.

QUOTE: MCC vice president: "This is a whole new way of doing business. This pooling of intellectual and financial resources is an idea whose time has come."

ISSUES: "Technology transfer is the weakest link in the chain," according to Admiral Inman, the MCC director. MCC has set up liaison personnel with each company to facilitate transfers, but the "not invented here" attitude will have to be overcome. Another issue is pressure toward keeping new knowledge and results proprietary, even among participating companies. Many shareholders are competitors. Some have invested in one program and not another, and the sums invested are relatively large. Also still to be evolved is the relationship with the University of Texas. The MCC defines the relationship as an "informal" web of projects, adjunct faculty, internships, and research funding. The University of Texas considers the MCC a future drawing card for new talent and resources in the post-oil era.

QUOTE: In March 1985, proposed cutbacks in the U.T. budget provoked Bobby Ray Inman to say, "If we were making the site selection in the spring of 1985 instead of the spring of 1983, I would have to think very carefully about whether I would recommend coming to Texas."

MICROELECTRONICS CENTER OF NORTH CAROLINA (MCNC)

Location	Research Triangle Park, North Carolina
Focus	Submicron silicon semiconductor manufacturing technology
Founded	July 1980 Opened October 1983

Funding

  Government $82 million since 1980 (through June 1987) (includes $40 million in related university investments)
(plus a $6.5 million microwave 150-mile system)

  Other $15 million external funding (through Jan. 86)

  Operating $18-20 million/year

  Companies   *Industrial affiliate*: $250,000 for each of three years, equipment or cash payments
Associate: ± $100,000/yr for each of 3 years, no full-time company staff involved at MCNC, only specialized involvement in company's field of expertise allowed
Sponsor: Acknowledged corporate donor of equipment and/or materials

Partners

  State Government

  Companies (10)

                        Affiliates:
       Airco Industrial Gases
       GCA/IC Systems
       General Electric Company
       IBM
       Monsanto
       Northern Telecom
       Shipley Associates
      Associates:
       Aeronca Electronics
       Allied Chemicals
       Convex Computer

MCNC (continued)

Universities (5 involving 23 departments)	Duke University North Carolina A&T State University North Carolina State University University of North Carolina at Chapel Hill University of North Carolina at Charlotte
Research Institute (1 involving 7 departments)	Research Triangle Institute
As of January 1986	D.S. Beilman, president 150 microelectronics science professionals 40 computer science professionals 60 electronic materials researchers 30 faculty recruited from industry (118 of the above are full time staff) 200 staff at associated institutions involved in microelectronics

Its short life—MCNC is only five years old—argues the huge benefits to be derived from a *sound, visionary, and non-intrusive public dollar* and from a *dedicated and broadly based constituency* of business people, academics, and politicians committed to a long-term agenda. It demonstrates, also, that while the initial corporate dollar investment in the MEC appears small, the overall corporate investment has been immense if one counts adjacent plant construction, job training, and the sharing of research facilities such as GE's $100 million commitment that includes brand new semiconductor laboratories and fabrication facilities.

POSITIVES: Like the CIS at Stanford, the MCNC represents the very best of what can be expected of an R&D consortium in the United States. Far beyond its original expectations, it has achieved three primary goals: (1) building a world-class research facility with an emphasis on commercial technology transfer, (2) catalyzing the collective efforts of dispersed academic and industry researchers while reinforcing the state's university research and educational infrastructure, and (3) acting as a magnet for the expansion of technologically intensive firms. All sectors of the economy, indeed of the national economy, have gained from the partnership. A working style has been created that encourages sharing of facilities, services, and people among participants. Not to be overlooked is the importance of sensitive and well-designed architecture that enhances the intended working style (see also CIS and CIDMAC on this point).

MCNC (continued)

ISSUES: One stands out. Small business involvement is limited at this time. This is due in part to a paucity of small high tech in the vicinity but also to the high entry price. By intent, the MCNC has limited corporate entry to large companies with complementary and noncompeting commercial interest. To date the MCNC only has seven major funding partners and a few other associated companies looking in on its research.

QUOTE from James Dykes, vice president and general manager GE Semiconductor Division: "There's a cooperative dialogue going on here with government and universities none of us had seen before."

ROBOTICS INSTITUTE (RI)

Location	Carnegie-Mellon University Pittsburgh, Pennsylvania
Focus	Automated manufacturing technologies
Founded	1979

Funding

Operating	$10 million/yr $5 million public sector and foundations (federal, state, NSF) $5 million industrial sponsors

Partners

University (1) Companies (28 sponsors and affiliates—the list changes)	Carnegie-Mellon University Advanced Robotics Corporation Aerotech Corporation Aluminum Corporation of America American Robot Corporation Commodore Business Machines Continental Group Contraves-Goerz Corporation Denning Mobile Robotics, Inc. Digital Equipment Corporation Dravo Corporation General Motors Corporation H.J. Heinz Company Hillman Company IBM Corporation Industrial Programming, Inc. International Cybernetics Corporation Mine Safety Appliance Company 3M Company Northern Telecom of Canada, Ltd. Oberg Manufacturing Company Rockwell International Corporation Siemens Corporation Sperry Corporation Sutherland, Sproull & Associates, Inc.

RI (continued)

The Systems Consulting Group
Travenol Laboratories, Inc.
Westinghouse Electric Corporation
Xerox Corporation

As of January 1986

Prof. Raj Reddy, director
35 affiliated faculty
25 research scientists
45 research engineers
60 graduate and undergraduate researchers

The Institute is committed to pursuing a full spectrum of research topics affecting the factory of the future. The work tends to be project specific. The result is a direct transfer of technology to sponsors. One of its *strengths is inherited from a campus culture* that discourages departmental barriers. In addition it has leveraged a vital resource: an unusually strong computer science faculty. This has been built up over the years with substantial help from the federal government (DARPA). The Institute is in many ways a one-stop supermarket of ideas in robotics and automated manufacturing. This has significant implications for sponsors and affiliates who can look in on the very latest developments and tap them with relative ease for development. The Institute is playing a direct role in stimulating revival of local and national companies. Pittsburgh-based Westinghouse is its biggest sponsor-client.

POSITIVES: A primary asset of the Institute is the cross-disciplinary approach resulting from an absence of departmental hierarchies. The large number of faculty and researchers associated with the Institute is testimony to campus-wide pervasiveness. Similarly, a reading of projects in process confirms a working belief in cross-disciplinary research. Another strength of the Institute is its ability to attract and retain large and small companies as sponsors or affiliates. State funds (provided through the Ben Franklin program) has allowed small companies to buy in as observers. This is highly significant if one considers the dilemma of the MCNC (and other consortia) and the visible absence of small companies.

RI (continued)

ISSUES: The principal negative is beyond the Institute's control. Larger corporate clients do not automatically mean predictable or long-term funding streams. This imposes serious burdens on the institute's budgets if research must be sustained after a client unexpectedly drops out (as did a subsidiary of Westinghouse that was sold to another company). Second, although there is a lot of talk of involving the nontechnical academic into its work, the number of faculty from the humanities remains small.

ROBOTICS RESEARCH CENTER (RRC)

Location	University of Rhode Island Kingston, Rhode Island
Focus	Research on "robots with vision"
Founded	Spring 1971 First funding of URI robotics research from NSF Research Initiation Grant
1975	Full funding from NSF for robotic vision research component
1980	Formal start of Industrial Participation program (IPP) with three companies: Unimation, Cheeseborough Ponds, and Textron
1981	Approximately 24 companies on board by end of summer
1982	NSF initiated University/Industry Cooperative Research Center in Robotics (UICR)

Funding

NSF $1.1 million (1975) over ten years; $.7 million (1982) over 4 years

YEAR:	82–83	84–85	85–86
NSF	$401,000	$192,000	$112,000
Companies	$520,000	$225,000	$250,000
@ $25,000 per year			$100,000 (AT&T project)
State	_____	$122,000	$122,000
Totals	$921,000*	$539,000	$584,000

* Note: URI officials report this as the official funding level. With equipment and university support, it exceeded $1 million

RRC (continued)

Partners

Government	The National Science Foundation
	State of Rhode Island
Academic Institution (1)	University of Rhode Island
Companies (10 as of 1/86)	Allied Corp.
	AT&T Technologies Corp.
	Barry Wright
	Brown & Sharpe
	Cheeseborough Ponds
	Ford Motor Company
	General Motors Corp.
	Honeywell
	IBM
	Rogers Corp.
As of January 1986	Professor Palm is director of the RRC.
	Dr. Boothroid is the director of the Advanced Manufacturing Institute: consisting of the RRC and the Center for Design for Manufacturability.
	29 RRC staff
	7 faculty (ME & EE Depts.)
	16 graduate students (3 Ph.D.s, 13 master's)
	3 undergraduates
	2 research associates
	1 lab technician

The National Science Foundation has been the largest single supporter of robotics research at URI. The NSF started funding the Center in 1971 and since that time their support in two programs has totalled $1.8 million. A decade later, there were more than twenty companies participating in the Industrial Participation Program with a major objective of being a world-class center for "robotics with vision." At present, shrinking support has caused serious cutbacks, but a new director, new facilities, and a new emphasis on manufacturing engineering may pull the consortium out of a consolidation mode.

RRC (continued)

POSITIVE: The RRC was one of the first robotics institutes in the country and provided a model for others. Its fifteen year progression from individual research projects to a university-industry consortium with a structured agenda backed by NSF support has allowed it to weather a discontinuity of personnel, uneven funding, and changes in research focus. Its interdisciplinary focus includes electrical, mechanical, and industrial engineering, as well as business administration. Technology transfer has taken place: Two industrial partners now license, use, and sell products patented at the RRC. Seven project leaders are supporting twenty projects. Several program researchers are internationally recognized. A new Applied Engineering Laboratory is being built to consolidate robotics research from three departments into one center. Industry participants worked with the dean of engineering to recruit a new Center director and write his job description.

ISSUES: The program director reports to the College of Engineering. This set-up forces the Center to compete in the URI structure for limited resources, space and personnel. In 1982, the dean of the College and director of the Center left for industry jobs, creating a leadership vacuum. NSF funding is winding down. The number of participating companies has declined. While the state picked up some of the budgetary slack, the failure of the "Greenhouse Compact" referendum—a state bond issue for technology development—limits the likelihood of long-term state support.

Some industrial participants dropped out because of a mismatch of agendas. Partly as a result, the Center is now consolidating and positioning its robotics research in a larger context of manufacturing processes. The new dean sees this as a bold move into generic research around "design for manufacturability." But the jury is still out. Whether the new focus can serve the short-term needs and expectations of the industrial partners is the new director's toughest challenge.

QUOTE from an NSF evaluator: "The problem with the partnership is that if it's hot, industry will buy away the dean and director of the program, like they did here."

QUOTE from an industrial participant: "Rhode Island is probably one of the closest in bringing new products to fruition. But if you are looking for a long term MIT solution, you won't find it here."

Appendix B
Equipment List
Center for Interactive Computer Graphics
Rensselaer Polytechnic Institute

1. INSTALLED EQUIPMENT
(Eight Major Computer Systems)

Cost Center (Instructional-General Research):

- 2 PRIME 750's (8MB Memory, 2400MB Disk), 2 800/1600 BPI Tapes, 600 LPM Line Printer, Card Reader
- PRIMENET Network with 2 *P750 & P500
- 36 IMLAC 6220 VECTOR REFRESH
- VERSATEC 1200A Electrostatic Plotter (11″), CALCOMP 1051 4-Color Pen (36″) Plotter, CALCOMP 5200 Electrostatic (11″), TEKTRONIX 4663 2-Pen Plotter (21″)
- 40″ × 30″ TALOS Digitizing Tablet
- 3 IMLAC DYNAGRAPHIC SERIES-II Vector Refresh
- TEKTRONIX 4113 Color Raster (640 × 480 × 4)
- TEKTRONIX 4115 Color Raster (1280 × 1024 × 8)
- 4341-12 (16MB Memory, 7500MB Disk), 3203 Line Printer
- (Channel Attached to IBM 4341-2, below), 3705
- 17 IBM 3250 Vector Terminals
- 8 IBM 5080 Raster Terminals
- 17 IBM 3178 A/N Terminals
- 6 IBM 3279 Raster Terminals
- 1 IBM 4250 Erosion Printer

Graphics and CAD/CAM Research System:

- IBM 4341-2 (8MB Memory, 4900 MB Disk), 2 1600/6250 BPI Tapes, 3203 Line Printer
- 2 IBM 3250 Vector Terminals, 3 IBM 3277 GA Storage Tube, 2 IBM 3279 Raster, 4 3278 Alphanumeric Terminals
- 6670 Laset Printer/Plotter (SHERPA-APA)
- 2 TEKTRONIX Hard Copy Units
- 2 ADAGE 4370 3D Vector Workstations
- 4 IBM Personal computers (128K Bytes Memory, 320KB Floppy Disks), EPSON 80 Printers, Color Monitors
- EVANS AND SUTHERLAND PS300 3D Vector Workstation
- 4 IBM 3277 Alphanumeric Terminals
- 2 IBM Device Attachment Control Units (DACU)
- IBM 5080 Raster Terminal
- IBM SERIES 1 (256KB Memory, 64MB Disk, 16 Async Communication Lines)

Raster Graphics, Database, Expert Systems:

- PRIME 500 (2MB Memory, 300MB Disk)
- 2 ADI Light 50 Color Raster (512 × 512 × 8)
- SANDERS Graphics 8-Color Raster (1024 × 1024 × 4)
- ELOGRAPHICS Touch Screen
- LEXIDATA 3400 Color Raster (640 × 512 × 10)
- 6 RASTER TECHNOLOGIES MODEL 1 Color Raster (512 × 512 × 24)
- DUNN 631 Color Camera System (35mm, 16mm, 8 × 10 POLAROID), MATRIX QCR D2000 Film Recorder
- BRITTON-LEE IDM 500 Base System with 1/2M Memory, Disk Controller, 300MB Disk
- ADAGE 3000 Raster Terminal (1024 × 1024 × 32)
- TEXTRONIX 4115 Color Raster (1280 × 1040 × 8)
- DATA GENERAL MV10000 (6MB, 100MB Disk) With GW4000 Workstation, GDC1000 Workstation, 8 A/N Terminals, 1600/6250 TAPE
- GENIGRAPHICS Film Recorder

Graphics and Hardware Research:

- HP 1000 F-SERIES (2MB Memory, 120MB Disk) 1600 BPI Taper, Line Printer
- 2 HP 2621A A/N Terminals, 1 2623P Terminal
- 2 HP 2648A Graphics Terminals
- HP 1351A Graphics Generator, 1310B Vector Display, 9111A Graphics Tablet
- GERBER IDS-80 Turnkey System on HP 1000 E-Series Satellite Processor (Tablet, Hardcopy Unit)
- HP 9872C 8-Color Pen Plotter (14″ × 19″)
- HP 64000 Microprocessor, Workstation with Local Mass Storage, 16MB Winchester Disk, Line Printer, Logic Analyzer, Prom Programmer and Emulator
- IBM SYSTEM 9000 Instrumentation Computer
- 2 IMLAC 6210

Beta-Site Equipment:

- MOSAIC Workstation

2. INSTALLED MAJOR APPLICATIONS SOFTWARE

- CADAM™,[a] 3D CADAM™ (Beta Site)
- CATIA™[b]
- NCAD™[c]
- GDP (Geometric Design Processor, IBM Experimental Solids)
- PADL 1 (University of Rochester Solid Geometry)
- CSMP III
- SPICE (Circuit Analysis)
- AD 2000 (1975 NASA IPAD Version)
- DYNAMIC CONTROL SYSTEMS (NASA ORACLS, UMIST Inverse NYQUIST)
- IGS (IBM Internal VLSI Layout)
- RIM (NASA IPAD Relational Database Manager)
- IBM 500 Database Query Language
- ANSYS (Finite Element)
- SPAR
- ABACUS
- SAP IV
- GERBER IDS-80 Turnkey CAD/CAM Software
- CAEDS (SDRC FEM Software)
- IMP (Integrated Mechanics Program, 1975 Wisconsin Version)
- GIAM (Graphics Interactive Applications Monitor)
- OPS5
- SQL (DATA GENERAL)

3. INSTALLED SYSTEMS/GRAPHICS SOFTWARE

Systems Software:

- PRIME PRIMOS V
- IBM VM/CMS, OSVS1, MVS
- IBM SERIES 1 EDX, RPS
- HP 1000 RTE 4B
- DG AOS/VS, UNIX

[a]CADAM™ is a registered trademark of CADAM, Inc.
[b]CATIA™ is a registered trademark of Dassault Systems
[c]NCAD™ is a registered trademark of Northrop Corporation

Graphics Software:

- IMLAC HGP, RGS, VC/IC (Beta Site)
- TEKTRONIX Plot 10, IGL
- HP Graphics 1000/II AGP/DGL
- IBM 3250 GSP/GAM
- RASTER TECH FORTRAN Support Package
- IBM 3279 GDDM
- EVANS AND SUTHERLAND
- IBM 3277 Gas
- Device Independent BELL NORTHERN VGM
- SANDERS Graphic 8 FSP/GCP
- ADAGE GPOTS/GPL

Appendix C
Sample Agreement
CIS—Stanford University

STANFORD UNIVERSITY CENTER FOR INTEGRATED SYSTEMS
COMPANY PARTICIPATION AGREEMENT

This participation agreement ("AGREEMENT") is entered into by:

_____

_____

_____

_____

(name and address of participating organization)

hereinafter "COMPANY", and The Board of Trustees of the Leland Stanford Junior University, Stanford, California 94305 ("STANFORD") which operates the Center for Integrated Systems ("CIS").

CIS is partially funded by the "CIS Gift Fund." Contributions from industrial sponsor companies for membership in and support of CIS form the "CIS Gift Fund."

In order to implement the CIS policy governing disposition of intellectual property rights arising out of CIS activities and to help assure the mutual benefits to the parties arising from AGREEMENT including those accruing to COMPANY as a result of its participation in CIS and association with STANFORD and those accruing to STANFORD as a result of association with COMPANY, and the parties agree as follows:

A. DESCRIPTION OF PARTICIPATION

STANFORD will permit employee(s) of and/or consultant(s) to COMPANY ("CIS VISITING SCIENTIST(S)"), as designated by mutual agreement between STANFORD and COMPANY, to participate in activities and use facilities of CIS during the period of AGREEMENT, and will inform CIS VISITING SCIENTIST of STANFORD's obligations to third parties under SPONSORED PROJECTS (as defined in Clause D(3)(b)) in which CIS VISITING SCIENTIST wishes to participate.

B. PERSONNEL RELATIONSHIPS

During all operations and activities of CIS VISITING SCIENTIST in association with CIS under AGREEMENT, CIS VISITING SCIENTIST shall be considered to be an employee of COMPANY, which is an independent contractor in relation to STANFORD. COMPANY shall obtain agreements from each CIS VISITING SCIENTIST as necessary to effectuate the provision of AGREEMENT. Similarly, STANFORD shall obtain agreements from each STANFORD employee and student as necessary to effectuate the provisions of AGREEMENT.

C. PAYMENT OF EXPENSES

CIS VISITING SCIENTIST will continue to receive his/her regular salary or other remuneration in accordance with terms and conditions of relationship with COMPANY. However, any expense incurred by CIS VISITING SCIENTIST at STANFORD's request will be paid by STANFORD.

D. INVENTIONS AND PATENTS

(1) *Definition of Invention*

An "Invention" under this AGREEMENT is any invention, whether or not patentable, conceived or discovered while participating in the activities of CIS, or using the facilities of CIS during the period of AGREEMENT.

(2) *Invention Identification, Disclosures and Reports*

Promptly upon conception or discovery, CIS VISITING SCIENTIST will prepare a full written disclosure of each Invention conceived or discovered by CIS VISITING SCIENTIST solely or jointly with others, specifically identifying the feature or concept which is believed to be novel, unobvious and useful, and including pertinent background information, using STANFORD Invention Disclosure Form SP-101, appended hereto as Appendix A.

Copies of such disclosure will be submitted promptly to STANFORD through the Associate Director, Intellectual Property Administration, Sponsored Projects Office, and to COMPANY. Copies of such disclosure and background information will also be forwarded promptly to the Office of Technology Licensing at STANFORD.

CIS VISITING SCIENTIST shall maintain laboratory notebooks or equivalent records adequate to serve as history of activities at CIS for both technical and patenting purposes.

Upon receiving a disclosure from any STANFORD employee or student of any Invention made by them under CIS projects in which CIS VISITING SCIENTIST is participating, STANFORD shall promptly notify and fully disclose the Invention to COMPANY, using STANFORD Invention Disclosure Form SP-101.

185

STANFORD and COMPANY shall hold each disclosure in confidence until filing of patent application thereon, but not for a period greater than 90 days from completion of disclosure.

(3) *Disposition of Rights in Inventions*

(a) *Inventions Made Under "CIS Gift Fund"*

All Inventions made solely under support from the CIS Gift Fund shall be placed in the public domain by publication.

(b) *Inventions Made Under Stanford Sponsored Projects*

COMPANY acknowledges that STANFORD accepts funds for, and enters into agreements for, the performance of research with numerous different entities, both public and private ("SPONSORED PROJECTS"). COMPANY further acknowledges that the relevant provisions of the agreement(s) for SPONSORED PROJECTS may obligate or permit STANFORD to take title to, to license, and/or convey title to Inventions conceived or first actually reduced to practice under SPONSORED PROJECTS.

STANFORD acknowledges that COMPANY intends that CIS VISITING SCIENTIST shall not perform any work under SPONSORED PROJECTS which precludes COMPANY from obtaining a license as provided in Paragraph D(4)(b) below, and agrees to inform CIS VISITING SCIENTIST of such SPONSORED PROJECTS.

COMPANY and STANFORD agree that rights in any Invention made under a SPONSORED PROJECT shall be governed by the relevant provision(s) of the agreement(s) for such SPONSORED PROJECTS.

(c) *Unsponsored Inventions Made with Use of CIS Facilities*

Rights in all Inventions made with the use of CIS facilities, and not made under SPONSORED PROJECTS or under "CIS Gift Fund," shall remain with the inventor(s) subject to his/her obligations to COMPANY or STANFORD or third parties.

(d) *Unpatented Inventions*

No rights shall be asserted by either party against the other with respect to Inventions which are not patented.

(4) *Inventions of CIS Visiting Scientists Under Projects Sponsored by the U.S. Government*

    (a) *Definition of CIS Subject Invention*

For the purpose of this Clause (4), CIS Subject Invention'' is any Invention made solely or jointly by CIS VISITING SCIENTIST in the performance of work under, and subject to a STANFORD grant or contract with the U.S. Government.

    (b) *Licenses*

Subject to any limitations referenced in Clause D(3)(b) above STANFORD hereby grants to COMPANY a license to each CIS Subject Invention on which patent application is filed. All such licenses are to be at least nonexclusive and royalty–free with the right to make, have made, use, have used, lease, sell and/or otherwise transfer any product, practice and have practiced any method, and sublicense COMPANY's affiliates and, to the extent necessary to fulfill any licensing including cross–licensing obligations of COMPANY in effect at date of issuance of letters patent of issuance of letters patent of the CIS Subject Invention, third parties.

COMPANY's affiliates herein means any entity at least 50% the stock or voting right of which is directly or indirectly owned or controlled by COMPANY or which directly or indirectly owns or controls at least 50% of the stock or voting rights of the COMPANY.

STANFORD shall forward a confirmatory license to COMPANY (and to the U.S. Government) for each CIS Subject Invention upon receipt of the Serial Number and Application Date for the patent application.

E. LIMITATIONS, WARRANTIES, INDEMNITY AND LIABILITY

Except as provided in Paragraph D(4)(b), no license is granted or implied by either party to the other under any patents now or hereafter obtained, nor will the furnishing of any information, programs or other material constitute any representation, warranty, assurance, guarantee or inducement by either party that the use of such information, programs or other material is free from infringement of any patent or copyright of others.

EACH PARTY MAKES NO WARRANTIES, EXPRESS OR IMPLIED, TO THE OTHER PARTY AS TO ANY MATTER WHATSOEVER, INCLUDING WITHOUT LIMITATION THE QUALITY OF THE RE-SEARCH OR ANY Invention(S) OR PRODUCT(S) WHETHER TANGI-BLE OR INTANGIBLE, CONCEIVED, DISCOVERED, OR DEVEL-OPED UNDER THIS AGREEMENT: OR THE OWNERSHIP, MER-CHANTABILITY, OR FITNESS FOR 'A PARTICULAR PURPOSE OF THE RESEARCH OR ANY SUCH Invention OR PRODUCT. STANFORD AND COMPANY WILL NOT BE LIABLE FOR ANY DIRECT, CONSE-QUENTIAL, OR OTHER DAMAGES SUFFERED BY ANY LICENSEE OR ANY OTHERS RESULTING FROM THE USE OF THE RESEARCH OR ANY SUCH Invention OR PRODUCT, AND NOTICE TO THIS EFFECT WILL BE INCLUDED IN ALL LICENSES GRANTED BY STANFORD.

Each party shall not be liable for any failure to perform as required by this AGREEMENT, to the extent such failure to perform is caused by any reason beyond the party's control, including failure of any governmental approval required for full performance.

F. ARBITRATION

The parties agree to submit all unresolved disputes arising between the parties in connection with this AGREEMENT, including rights in any Invention made in the course of CIS projects in which CIS VISITING SCIENTIST participated, to arbitration in accordance with the Rules of Conciliation and Arbitration or, wherever applicable, the Patent Arbitration Rules of the American Arbitration Association. The parties further agree that the arbitration decision shall be binding and conclusive to the parties.

G. LIMITATION ON ASSIGNMENT OF AGREEMENT

Neither party will assign this AGREEMENT to another without the prior written consent of the other party; however, COMPANY may assign this AGREEMENT to a successor in ownership of all or substantially all its business assets. Such successor will expressly assume in writing the obligation to perform in accordance with the terms and conditions of this AGREEMENT. Any other purported assignment will be void.

H. NONDISCRIMINATION

STANFORD and COMPANY will not discriminate against any CIS VISITING SCIENTIST because of race, color, religion, sex, or national origin.

I. GOVERNING LAW AND CONSENT TO JURISDICTION

AGREEMENT shall be governed by and construed in accordance with the laws of the State of California. STANFORD and COMPANY hereby expressly and irrevocably agree that all actions or claims to enforce the provisions of AGREEMENT shall be in the State of California. With respect to any action or claim arising under this AGREEMENT COMPANY hereby irrevocably consents to personal jurisdiction in the appropriate state court in California or federal court therein, and to service of process in accordance with the provisions of the laws of the State of California.

J. MORE FAVORABLE TERMS

STANFORD represents that AGREEMENT is the common understanding between STANFORD and companies participating in CIS and that licensing rights granted to COMPANY by STANFORD under this AGREEMENT are not less favorable than those under other existing CIS Company Participation Agreements.

Upon STANFORD entering a subsequent CIS Company Participation Agreement which bears more favorable licensing rights and terms than those in this AGREEMENT, such licensing terms of the subsequent CIS Company Participation Agreement shall be offered to COMPANY in lieu of the licensing terms in this AGREEMENT.

K. SEVERABILITY

If any provisions of AGREEMENT or the application of any such provision shall be held by a tribunal of competent jurisdiction to be invalid or unenforceable, the remaining provisions of AGREEMENT shall remain in full force and effect.

L. SCOPE

AGREEMENT contains the entire understanding between the parties with respect to the participation in the activities and use of CIS facilities by CIS VISITING SCIENTISTS and the disposition of rights in intellectual properties conceived or created by CIS VISITING SCIENTISTS in his/her activities at CIS. No amendments or changes to AGREEMENT will be effective unless made in writing and signed by authorized representatives of STANFORD and COMPANY.

M. TERM OF AGREEMENT

AGREEMENT shall be effective upon COMPANY becoming a member of CIS by making an annual contribution to the "CIS Gift Fund" and shall terminate upon COMPANY terminating its membership in CIS. However, any license granted under this AGREEMENT before termination or grantable at termination shall survive the termination of AGREEMENT.

Accepted and agreed to:

COMPANY _____
(organization name)

By _____ Title _____

Signature _____ Date _____

THE BOARD OF TRUSTEES
OF THE LELAND STANFORD JUNIOR UNIVERSITY

By _____ Title _____

Signature _____ Date _____

Appendix D
Sample Agreement
RI—Carnegie-Mellon University

This contract sets forth the terms and conditions of an Agreement between Carnegie-Mellon University (CMU) and *Corpname* whereby CMU will conduct work tasks and render services to *Corpname* subject to the following terms and conditions.

1. *SCOPE OF WORK*

CMU will perform research in accordance with Attachment A.

2. *RESPONSIBILITIES OF THE PARTIES*

a. *Corpname* agrees to:

   i. Make payment to CMU for services provided under this Agreement and on a schedule set forth in Attachment A.

b. CMU agrees to:

   i. Perform the work and services described in Attachment A of this Agreement.

   ii. Provide reports on at least a semi-annual basis, of the results of carrying out the research described in Attachment A.

   iii. Afford *Corpname* all the rights and privileges accorded Industrial Affiliates.

3. *TERM*

The term of this Agreement shall be for a period of *Corpname/time* commencing on the date of acceptance of this Agreement by CMU.

4. *CONFIDENTIAL INFORMATION*

Neither party shall disclose or receive any confidential information other than pursuant to a separate Confidential Disclosure Agreement mutually agreed to by the parties. In the event any Confidential Information is transferred to advance the project, it shall be done so pursuant to a separate Confidential Disclosure Agreement mutually agreed to by the parties.

5. *PUBLICATIONS AND COPYRIGHTS*

CMU will be free to publish the results of research under this Agreement. At least sixty (60) days prior to such publication CMU shall submit the publication to *Corpname* for review. *Corpname* shall review such publication to determine whether either *Corpname* confidential information or patentable or copyrightable materials would be disclosed in such publication. If

Corpname determines that either *Corpname* confidential information of patentable or copyrightable materials would be disclosed in such publication *Corpname* will notify CMU of this within thirty (30) days of *Corpname*'s receipt of the publication from CMU. In such event *Corpname* and CMU will, within (30) days of such notification by *Corpname* agree upon revisions to the publication that will avoid disclosure of *Corpname* confidential information or patentable or copyrightable materials.

Reports submitted to *Corpname* in accordance with the workscope hereunder shall be the property of *Corpname*. However, title to and the right to determine the disposition of any copyrights, or material on which a copyright may be obtained, first produced or composed in the performance of this research, shall remain with CMU subject to a grant by CMU to *Corpname* of an irrevocable, royalty-free, worldwide, nonexclusive license to use, execute, reproduce, display, perform, distribute, prepare derivative works thereof, and to authorize others to do any, some or all of the foregoing.

6. *WARRANTY*

CMU warrants, the originality of the work prepared under this Agreement and that no portion of such work or its use or distribution by *Corpname* or CMU, violates or is protected by any copyright, patent, trade secret, or similar proprietary right of any third party.

7. *DISCLOSURES*

"Invention" shall mean any invention, discovery, or improvement, whether or not patentable, conceived or first actually reduced to practice, by CMU or CMU's employees or students and either with or without one or more employees of *Corpname* during the term of this Agreement and in the performance of services hereunder. CMU shall promptly make a complete written disclosure of each invention, specifically pointing out the features or concepts which CMU believes to be new or different.

8. *PATENT RIGHTS*

a. Ownership and License of Inventions

Each Invention, other than an Invention made jointly by one or more employees of CMU with one or more employees of *Corpname*, shall be CMU's property except as otherwise provided herein, subject to a license which CMU hereby grants to *Corpname*. CMU shall notify *Corpname* promptly as to each country in which CMU elects to seek protection by obtaining patent rights, at CMU's expense, or that CMU elects not to seek such protection. CMU shall promptly seek such protection in each said elected country.

Each invention made jointly by one or more employees of CMU with one or more employees of *Corpname* or each invention made solely by one or more employees of *Corpname* shall be *Corpname* property.

If CMU elects to seek such protection on said Invention only in certain countries, *Corpname* and/or its designee shall have the right to seek such protection, at its expense, on said Invention in any and all neglected countries. Title to all patents issued thereon shall vest in the party seeking such protection. The party filing such applications shall promptly provide the other party with a copy of each application so filed and, upon request, copies of all official papers relating thereto.

If CMU seeks such protection on said Invention in any country, CMU agrees to grant and hereby grants *Corpname* a license, under any and all patents issuing on applications CMU files on said Invention. If *Corpname* and/or its designee seeks such protection on said Invention in any nonelected country, then *Corpname* agrees, upon request, to cause to be granted to CMU, a license under any and all patents issued on applications and/or its designee files on such Invention.

If CMU elects not to seek such protection on an Invention in any country whatsoever, CMU shall promptly notify *Corpname* and *Corpname* and/or its designee shall have the right to seek such protection on said Invention and title to said Invention and title to all patents issued thereon shall vest in *Corpname* and/or its designee, subject to a license which hereby agrees, upon request, to be caused to be granted to CMU. In the event that CMU elects not to seek such protection in any country, *Corpname* shall also have the right to publish such Invention.

b. CMU shall, upon *Corpname*'s request and at *Corpname*'s expense, cause patent applications to be filed thereon, through solicitors designated by *Corpname*, and forthwith assign all such applications to *Corpname* its successors and assigns. CMU shall give *Corpname* and its solicitors all reasonable assistance in connection with the preparation and prosecution of any such patent applications and shall cause to be executed all such assignments and other instruments and documents as *Corpname* may consider necessary or appropriate to carry out the intent of this Section.

c. To the extent that *Corpname* has the right to do so, *Corpname* hereby grants to CMU an irrevocable, nonexclusive, nontransferable and fully paid-up license throughout the world under any said Inventions assigned to *Corpname* pursuant to this Section hereof, and under any patents throughout the world issuing thereon including reissues, extensions, divisions and continuations thereof; *provided, however*, that such license is not applicable to any Inventions, patent applications arising out of any other inventions of either party.

9. *MEMBERSHIP IN THE INDUSTRIAL AFFILIATES PROGRAM*

a. The Affiliate shall have the right to receive royalty free non-exclusive licenses for the commercial development of all patents and copyrights obtained by Carnegie-Mellon University for work supported in whole or in part by funds from the Industrial Affiliates Program.

b. The Affiliate will receive all non-proprietary reports and documents published by the Institute.

c. The Affiliate will receive monthly reviews of the technical literature in the field of robotics.

d. The Affiliate will be eligible to attend bi-annual review of research in progress organized by the Institute.

e. The Affiliate may receive up to 12 hours of consultative service from the staff of the Institute, provided that:

i. the task is appropriate to the nature and level of expertise of the staff;

ii. all requests are directed to the program coordinator, and

iii. all expenses associated with the consultations will be paid by the Affiliate.

10. *GENERAL PROVISION*

a. The rights and obligations of Sections 4 thru 7, shall survive and continue after any expiration or termination of this Agreement and shall bind the parties and their legal representatives, successors, heirs, and assigns.

b. It is understood and agreed by the parties that CMU is retained as an independent contractor and in no event shall any employee or agent hired by CMU or any student, be or be considered an employee of *Corpname*. Matters governing the terms and conditions of employment of CMU's employees are entirely within the province of CMU. *Corpname* shall have no right to control any of the actions of the employees of CMU in such matters as work schedules, wage rates, worker's compensation, withholding income taxes, disability benefits, and the manner and means through which the work under this Agreement will be accomplished, such being entirely the responsibility of CMU.

11. *CMU'S FREEDOM TO PROVIDE SERVICES*

CMU represents and warrants that it is under no obligation or restriction, nor will, it assume any such obligation or restriction, which would in any way interfere with the services to be furnished by CMU under this Agreement.

12. *TERMINATION*

This Agreement may be terminated without cause by either party upon written notice at the end of any CMU academic semester or summer session provided such written notice is given at least thirty (30) days prior to the end of that semester or summer session. This Agreement may be terminated for cause by either party at any time.

13. *PENNSYLVANIA LAW*

This Agreement shall be construed, and the legal relations between the parties hereto shall be determined in accordance with the laws of the State of Pennsylvania.

ACCEPTED AND AGREED TO:

Corpname CORPORATION   Carnegie-Mellon University

By: _____ By: _____

Title: _____Title: _____

Date: _____ Date: _____

Index

About the Authors

Dan Dimancescu is an international consultant and writer on high-technology strategy and corporate management issues, and has authored and coauthored several books on technology policy and management topics. He is a senior lecturer at the Thayer School of Engineering and the Amos Tuck School of Business Administration, both at Dartmouth College, and a past lecturer at the Kennedy Institute of Politics, Harvard University.

James Botkin is a writer, researcher, and consultant on technology, management, and learning. He has authored and coauthored books on education and technology issues. He is a member of the Club of Rome, a former academic director of the Salzburg Seminar, and a former visiting faculty member at the Harvard School of Education.

Queries from the authors can be addressed care of TSG, 50 Church Street, Cambridge, Massachusetts, 02138.

Note: This book was set in Avant Garde and Times Roman typefaces. The manuscript was prepared on a Wang IOS System. It was then typeset on a Xyvision Electronic Publishing System by C&C Associates, Wilmington, Massachusetts. Type specifications, page layouts, and cover design are by Dan Dimancescu.